Notes on Music in Old Boston

AMS PRESS
NEW YORK

The TOWN of
BOSTON
IN
New England
by
Capt John Bonner
1722
Ætatis Suæ 60.
Charles River
Ferry to Charles Town
Bartons Point
Copper Works
Rope Walk
Mill Pond
EbN. Mill Damm
N. Water Mill
West Hill
Fox Hill
Beacon Hill
Powder House
Watch House
COMMON
Roxbury Flatts
School
Cornhill
Middle Street
Salem Street
North Street
Ship Street
N. Battery
Clarks Ship Yd
Scarletts Wharfe
Clarks Wharfe
Old Wharfe
Long Wharfe
Olivers Dock
Fort Hill
S. Battery
HARBOUR
Hills Wharfe
Wind Mill Point
Scale of a Mile.
BOSTON N.E.
Planted An. Dom. 1630
A. The Old Church 1630
B. Old North 1650
C. Old South 1669
D. Annabaptist 1680
E. Ch. of England 1688
F. Brattle St Church 1699
G. Quakers 1710
H. New North 1714
I. New South 1716
K. French 1716
L. New N. Brick 1721
EXPLANATION.
a. Town House
b. Governours House
c. South Grammar School
d. North Grammar School
e. Writing School
f. Writing School
g. Alms House
h. Bridewell
Streets 42 Lanes 36 Alleys 22
Houses near 3000
1000 Brick rest Timber
Near 12000 People.
Great Fires.
First 1653
Second 1676
Third 1679
Fourth 1683
Fifth 1690
Sixth 1691
Seventh 1702
Eigth 1711
Genll Small Pox.
First 1640
Second 1660
Third 1677 1678
Fourth 1690
Fifth 1702
Sixth 1721
Engraven and Printed by Fra. Dewing Boston N.E. 1722.

NOTES ON MUSIC IN OLD BOSTON

BY
WILLIAM ARMS FISHER

BOSTON
OLIVER DITSON COMPANY
1918

Library of Congress Cataloging in Publication Data

Fisher, William Arms, 1861-1948.
   Notes on music in old Boston.

   Reprint of the 1918 ed. published by O. Ditson,
Boston.
   Includes index.
   1. Music—Massachusetts—Boston. 2. Ditson (Oliver)
Company, Inc., I. Title.
ML200.8.B7F4   1976   780.'9744'61   74-27340
ISBN 0-404-12914-5

Reprinted with permission of Theodore Presser Company

From the edition of 1918, Boston
First AMS edition published in 1976
Manufactured in the United States of America

AMS PRESS INC.
NEW YORK, N.Y.

ACKNOWLEDGMENT

IN the preparation of this book special acknowledgment is due to Mr. Walter Kendall Watkins, Secretary of the Society of Colonial Wars, for his invaluable knowledge regarding early Boston. The chapters on "Some Early Book and Music Shops" and the "Site of the Hay-Market Theatre" are due to his research.

Thanks are also due to Mr. Julius H. Tuttle of the Massachusetts Historical Society, Mr. Charles F. Read of the Bostonian Society, Mr. Otto Fleischner, Mr. Walter G. Forsyth and Miss Barbara Duncan of the Boston Public Library, and Miss Mary Alden Thayer of the Harvard Musical Association for courtesies extended.

The author is also indebted to Mr. Joseph M. Jennings of the Old Corner Bookstore, Mr. Edward McGlenen, City Registrar of Boston, Mr. J. M. Priaulx and Mr. H. J. Haney for illustrations, and to Mrs. George Whitefield Stone for the portrait of her grandfather, G. Graupner, and for information regarding him.

The author takes pleasure in acknowledging his indebtedness to the indispensable bibliographies of Mr. O. G. Sonneck on "Early Concert-Life in America" and "Early Secular American Music," and to that of Mr. Frank J. Metcalf on "American Psalmody."

W. A. F.

CONTENTS

	Page
Acknowledgment	vii
List of Illustrations	xi
Boston Common, a prefatory note	xiii
First Seventy Years, The	1
Eighteenth Century, The	6
Some Early Book and Music Shops	20
Nineteenth Century, The	30
Site of the Hay-Market Theatre	50
Fifty Years More	70
Chronology of the Oliver Ditson Company	76
Ditson Building, The	79
Index	ci

LIST OF ILLUSTRATIONS

Buildings, Views and Maps

	Page
Back Bay district in March, 1918, from Ditson Building	94
Beacon Hill and Boston Common in 1838 from intersection of the Providence and Worcester railroads	38
Beacon Street in March, 1918, from roof of Ditson Building	92
Bonner's Map of Boston in 1722	Frontispiece
Boston from Pemberton Hill in 1816, from the painting by Salmon	26
Boston Common and Vicinity in 1722, from Bonner's Map	49
Boston Common in 1804, from the painting by Dobbins	xiii
Boston Common and State House about 1820	30
Boston Common and State House in 1830, from the water-color by George Harvey	Title, 29
Boston Common and Public Garden about 1850, birdseye view	41
Colonnade Row, in 1844	67
Colonnade Row, in 1858	66
Colonnade Row, in 1860	65
Common Street (Tremont Street) in 1798, Robertson's view of	61
Common Street (Tremont Street) from West Street to Frog Lane, in 1800, from pencil drawing by George M. Woodward	50
Concert Hall, Hanover Street	16
Ditson Building, new, interior views	81–91
Ditson Buildings, various	37, 39, 40, 71, 72, 74–79, 96
Great Organ in Music Hall	45
Hatch Tavern, from pencil sketch by George M. Woodward	59
Hay-Market Theatre, from pencil sketch by George M. Woodward	59
Head Place and House, from pencil sketch by George M. Woodward	59
Hay-Market Theatre in 1798, Robertson's view of	61
Holden's Organ	13
House in Louisburg Square in which Jenny Lind was married	44
King's Chapel about 1865	33
Knot-Work, Title page of New Alphabet in, by Abiah Holbrook	56
New Winthrop House in 1852	67
Old Corner Bookstore about 1837	37

Buildings, Views and Maps

State House, old, from Cornhill (Washington Street) in 1791	19
State House, old, and State Street in 1801	20
State House, new, from roof of Ditson Building in March, 1918	95
Tremont Street from Colonial Building in March, 1918	96
Tremont Street from West Street to Boylston in March, 1918	93
Washington Street, West Side in 1845 (No. 107 to No. 135)	39

Music

Adams and Liberty, from *Boston Musical Miscellany*, 1815	62
Cambridge Short Tune, from *Bay Psalm Book*, 14th edition, 1709	4
Hollis Street, from Billings' *New England Psalm Singer*, 1770	12
Medfield Tune, from *New England Psalm Singer*, 1770	12
Windsor Tune, from *Bay Psalm Book*, 9th edition, 1698	4
Windsor Tune, from *Bay Psalm Book*, 14th edition, 1709	4
Windsor Tune, from Walter's *Grounds and Rules of Musick*, 1721	7
York Tune, from *Bay Psalm Book*, 9th edition, 1698	4
York Tune, from Walter's *Grounds and Rules of Musick*, 1721	7

Portraits

	Page		Page
Briggs, Edward W.	87	Healy, P. J.	70
Buck, Dudley	48	Higginson, Henry Lee	42
Carreño, Teresa, at ten	45	Holden, Oliver	13
Church, John	70	Lang, B. J.	46
Ditson, Charles H.	69	Lind, Jenny	44
Ditson, Oliver	68, 73	Paine, John K.	48
Dwight, John S.	43	Rudersdorff, Hermine	47
Eichberg, Julius	46	Urso, Camilla, at eleven	45
Graupner, Gottlieb	30	Vane, Sir Henry	2
Grisi, Giulia	44	Woodman, Clarence A.	89
Haynes, John C.	74	Zerrahn, Carl	42

BOSTON COMMON

A PREFATORY NOTE

THE buildings that face Boston Common look out upon open acres set in the very heart of a city that has grown great about them.

On or near the Common much of interest in American history has occurred, great men have walked there and near its borders great deeds have been done. To erect a new building overlooking it means more, therefore, than breaking the old sky-line, for it relates the new structure and the daily activities within it to an historic past rich in associations from which they cannot be detached.

The newest of these buildings houses the oldest music publishing concern in the United States. Its windows look west across the Common, over the even ranks of the Back Bay chimney-pots to the Charles River and to Cambridge beyond, with the tower of Harvard's Memorial Hall silhouetted against the remoter heights of Arlington.

Beneath its windows near the southeast corner of the Common begins the Long Path that leads to Joy Street, made unforgettable through the charm of the *Autocrat of the Breakfast Table;* and when Holmes was a youth of fifteen General Lafayette was escorted with pomp along the street below, a throng of school children on the Common welcoming the hero by singing *The Marseillaise,* one of the young singers being Wendell Phillips. Now the broad walk along the Tremont Street side of the Common is known as Lafayette Mall.

It may have been nine years earlier that young Emerson is remembered to have driven the family cow down Beacon Street along the Common to an adjoining pasture, for it was not until 1833 that cows were excluded on complaint of the ladies. The boys always have used and still claim part of the Common as a playground, and the man whose name is cut in the white marble front of this new building played there, too, a hundred years ago.

A little to the right in our window picture, on the knoll where the tall Soldiers' Monument stands, British artillery was stationed during the siege of Boston, and in the years preceding, British troops delighted in shocking religious Bostonians by racing horses on the Common on Sunday or causing their bands to play *Yankee Doodle* outside church doors.

The waters of the Back Bay once lapped the Common's marshy edge, and in the right of our window picture, where Blaxton had his wharf, the British troops, on the night of April 18, 1775, took their boats on the eve of the battle of Lexington, and with muffled oars rowed to the Cambridge shore; and in the little triangular burying ground close by are graves of British soldiers killed at Bunker Hill. Somewhere in the same enclosure is the unmarked grave of the patriot composer, William Billings.

Over yonder, across the Charles, when the provincial troops were quartered in the churches and college buildings of Cambridge, they took down the leaden window-weights and organ pipes of Christ Church to mould them into bullets used at Bunker Hill; and near this same church, on July 3, General Washington took command of the levies assembled there preparatory to the siege of Boston.

Directly across the Common, near the corner of Beacon and Spruce Streets, long ago stood the hut and orchard of the Hermit of Shawmut, the Rev. William Blaxton, the first inhabitant, and it was from him that the Town of Boston, in 1634, bought for £30 all his rights in the peninsula, reserving forty-four acres as

Commons for the freemen of the town for a "trayning field" and for "the feeding of cattell."

That the new home of the pioneer music publisher of the country should overlook Boston Common is altogether fitting, for in its vicinity were issued the first book printed in America, the first treatise on singing, the first printed music, the first music instruction book, and the first book wholly of American composition.

Not far from it the first singing school was held, the first organ erected, the first spinet built, the first public concert advertised, the pioneer orchestra organized, the first complete performance of an oratorio given, and at the northeastern corner of the Common, in Park Street Church, *My Country, 'tis of thee* was for the first time sung.

As inheritors of so significant a past, it would therefore be only right to acknowledge the debt by briefly noting some of the facts in the musical life of Boston, that link the olden days to the present.

Wm. Arms Fisher

Boston, February 22, 1918

THE FIRST SEVENTY YEARS

W HEN John Winthrop's company of Puritans found shelter in Boston harbor in June, 1630, they located on the mainland in Charlestown. The promontory of Shawmut was then occupied alone by a bookish recluse, the Rev. William Blaxton, "retaining no ſimbole of his former profeſſion but a Canonical Coate." He had built him a hut and planted an orchard on the southern slope of the Trimountaine. Almost on its site stands today at No. 48 Beacon Street a tall and solitary bachelor's apartment house.

In friendliness, well knowing that his cherished solitude was over, Blaxton visited the newcomers and invited them to establish themselves on the peninsula where there were goodly springs of water, the situation moreover being much better adapted for defence. The colonists accepted the invitation and on September 17, 1630, it was ordered "that Trimountaine shalbe called Boſton."

One of the first houses built was that of Mr. Isaac Johnson, a man of wealth and honorable lineage. This house was partly or entirely on the site of the building long occupied by the Old Corner Bookstore. Across the way were located the notables of the town: the governor, the elder of the church, the captain of the Artillery Company, and near by were the meeting-house, market and town-house, school-house, and the ever-flowing spring of pure water.

Four years after the settlement of Boston, William Hutchinson and his wife, Anne, arrived and came into possession of the Johnson estate. Anne Hutchinson's charitableness, superior mind, and force of character quickly gave her influence and drew to her many of the women and such prominent men as the Rev. John Cotton, her former pastor in England, and the young Governor, the brilliant Henry Vane, son of a privy councilor and high in the confidence of King Charles. Her independence of thought with her protests against the Puritanic legalism of the day divided the colony and brought about her banishment in 1638 "as being a woman not fit for our fociety." Cotton recanted, and Vane, defeated by Winthrop for the governorship at the election of 1637, returned to England in disgust. Today he is called to mind by MacMonnies' spirited statue which stands in the vestibule of the Boston Public Library.

In those days politics and theology were inseparable and to criticise official orthodoxy was dangerous. It was discontent with this autocracy that in 1638 led a large part of the population of New Towne (Cambridge), together with others from Dorchester and Watertown, to emigrate to Connecticut; and the first president of Harvard College, the Rev. Henry Dunster, was removed from office by this same autocracy for questioning infant baptism.

It was the bequest of the Rev. John Harvard that had changed an as yet unorganized school in 1638 into Harvard College, and the name of New Towne to Cambridge. In this town, now the home of the Riverside Press, the University Press, and the Athenæum Press, the first book issued in the colonies, with the exception of an almanac, was printed in 1640. This was the metrical version of the Psalms known as *The Bay Pfalm Book*. It contained no music, however. The five or six tunes then in use, when noted at all, were written in the back of the psalm books. Many congregations had but three or four tunes they could sing passably, for singing by rote was the custom, the Psalms being "lined out" by the deacon. A desire to better this condition was evidently felt by the Rev. John Cotton, who published in 1647 his tract, *Singing of Pfalms a Gofpel ordinance*, touching the duty itself, the matter to be sung, the singers, and the manner of singing.

If, as has been stated, music was printed about 1690 to be appended to the psalm books, no specimens have survived; and it was not until 1698 that the ninth edition of *The Bay Pfalm Book*, printed in Boston, contained thirteen tunes in two-part harmony. This crudely printed book, without bars except at the end of each line, is the oldest existing music of American imprint. The notes were cut on wood, which will explain in part the appearance of the page reproduced here at the left. A page from the fourteenth edition, issued in 1709, is given at the right. The later edition contains the melodies of twelve tunes. The notation of both *York Tune* and *Windsor Tune* may be compared with that given by Thomas Walter in the next chapter.

As an evidence of progress it should be noted that Brattle Square Church on December 20, 1699, "Voted unanimously that ye psalms in our public Worship be sung without Reading line by line."

About the only evidence that merry-hearted singing

4

and dancing were known in this early period is due to the fact that as a seaport Boston had many transient visitors, especially seamen, who indulged in such pleasure when ashore. Their conduct, made noisy no doubt by "much wafte of Wine and Beer," resulted, as early as 1646, in a law forbidding dancing in ordinaries and inns under penalty of five shillings for each offence.

In those days the very name "musician" was one of reproach, but stern as were the events and conditions of the period surely some mother-hearts crooned lullabies as they rocked the cradle, or over their housework hummed in soft undertone some unforgotten folksong.

The Colonial literature of the last half of the seventeenth century, mostly an arid waste of forbidding theology, reflects the sombreness of the period. At the same time the growing material prosperity, coupled with echoes from the reaction against Puritanism the Restoration had brought in, the establishment of the Church of England in Boston, the presence of an aristocratic official British class, and other influences, had a mellowing effect and bigotry gradually weakened.

THE EIGHTEENTH CENTURY

In 1700 Boston had become a thrifty town of growing prosperity, with a population of perhaps 7,000. Two years before the first music of American imprint had appeared and with the advent of printed music the "new way" of singing by note came in.

The first book issued to meet this new want was entitled: "*A very plain and eafy Introduction to the Art of Singing Pfalm Tunes:* With the Cantus, or Trebles, of Twenty-eight Pfalm Tunes contrived in such a manner as that the Learner may attain the Skill of Singing them with the greateft eafe and Speed imaginable. By Rev. Mr. John Tufts. Price, *6d.* or *5s.* the doz."

This little book of a few pages, the first American book of sacred music published, was issued in Boston in 1714 or 1715, and was so successful, in spite of its substitution of letters for notes, as to reach its eleventh edition in 1744.

The innovation of note singing raised a great tempest among the older people, who regarded it as a plan to shut them out from one of the ordinances of worship. It was bitterly objected to as "Quakerifh and Popifh, and introductive of inftrumental mufick; the names given to the notes are blafphemous; it is a needlefs way fince their good Fathers are gone to heaven without it; its admirers are a company of young upſtarts; they ſpend too much time about learning, and tarry out a-nights diſorderly," with many other equally strenuous and weighty reasons.

One of the valiant defenders of the "new way" was the Rev. Thomas Walter of Roxbury, who brought out in 1721, *The Grounds and Rules of Muſick explained, or an introduction to the art of ſinging by note.* This, the first practical American instruction book, and said to be the first music printed with bar-lines in America, was from the press of J. Franklin, at a time when his younger brother Benjamin, then a lad of fifteen, was learning the printer's trade as his apprentice.

Page, reduced, from Walter's "Grounds and Rules of Musick"

The gradual victory of the advocates of the "new way" led to the establishment of singing schools, and as early as 1717 one is said to have existed in Boston. Judge Sewall records in his diary, under the date

March 16, 1721: "At night Dr. Mather preached in the School-House to the young Musicians, from Rev. 14.3. 'No man could learn that Song.'—House was full, and the Singing extraordinarily Excellent, such as has hardly been heard before in Boston. Sung four times out of Tate and Brady."

The Rev. Cotton Mather, Sewall's uncle, wrote in his own diary of the same date: "In the Evening I preached unto a large Auditory, where a Society of persons learning to Sing, began a quarterly solemnity." It is interesting to remember that when a few venturesome Bostonians, at the risk of learning ungodly songs, first met to sing in a class together, the mighty Handel, under the patronage of George the First, was dominating London's musical life, and the modest Bach was living the quiet life of *Kapellmeister* to an obscure German prince.

The music, or rather, the psalm singing (for there was little else) was of course without the aid of instruments. When in 1713 Thomas Brattle, Esq., of Boston, willed the Brattle Square Church an organ, they declined it. He had provided, however, that in this event it was to be given to Queen's Chapel (known since the reign of Queen Anne as King's Chapel), but so great was the prejudice that the organ remained seven months in the porch of the church before it was unpacked. This instrument, set up in 1714, was the first pipe organ used in a church in the Colonies, and it was bitterly denounced by Dr. Cotton Mather and other dignitaries of the day. In 1733 the second organ in New England was set up in Trinity Church, Newport. In 1790 the Brattle Square Church, having taken seventy-seven years to change its mind, ordered an organ built in London, but even then one of its leading members offered to reimburse the church for its outlay and to give a sum to the poor of Boston if they would allow him to have the unhallowed instrument thrown into the harbor. As late as 1814 there was no organ in Park Street Church, Boston, the singing being supported by a flute, bassoon and 'cello. Thomas Ryan of the Mendelssohn Quintette Club, who came to Boston in 1845, played the clarinet for two years in Father Streeter's Church in Hanover Street, the other instruments being a double-bass and ophicleide. There was then, he records, no organ in this and several other Boston churches.

A growing interest in instrumental music is indicated by the advertisement of Mr. Edward Enstone, who came from England in 1714 to be the organist of King's Chapel, the second to occupy this position. The *Bofton News-Letter* of April 16-23, 1716, states: "This is to give notice that there is lately fent over from London a choice Collection of Mufickal Inftruments, confifting of Flageolets, Flutes, Haut-Boys, Bafs-Viols, Violins, Bows, Strings, Reads for Haut-Boys, Books of Inftructions for all thefe Inftruments, Books of ruled Paper. To be Sold at the Dancing School of Mr. Enftone in Sudbury Street near the Orange Tree, Bofton."

"NOTE. Any perfon may have all Inftruments of

Muſick mended, or Virgenalls and Spinnets Strung and Tuned at a reaſonable Rate, and likewiſe may be taught to Play on any of theſe Inſtruments above mention'd; dancing taught by a true and eaſier method than has been heretofore."

In 1764 Josiah Flagg of Boston, published *A Collection of the beſt Pſalm Tunes, in two, three and four-parts*, the largest collection up to this time printed in New England. This volume of about eighty small oblong pages is notable in that for the first time light music was intermingled with Psalm tunes, and because the music was engraved with skill by the noted silversmith, Paul Revere—and further, that it was printed on paper made in the colonies, which fact Mr. Flagg hopes "will not diminiſh the value of the work in the eſtimation of any, but may in ſome degree, recommend it, even to thoſe who have no peculiar reliſh for the muſic."

This Josiah Flagg was a man of energy and enthusiasm, and for some time the most important local musician. He gave concerts of quality, and as early as 1771 the name of Handel appears on his programs.

In 1769 the *Boſton Gazette* stated: "That a few days ſince was ſhipped for Newport a very curious Spinnet, being the firſt ever made in America, the performance of the ingenious Mr. John Harris of Boſton." Judging from his advertisement

From L O N D O N,
JOHN HARRIS,
WHO arrived in Capt. Calef, begs leave to inform the public, that he MAKES and SELLS all ſorts of HARPSICHORDS AND SPINNETS. Likewiſe mends, repairs, new ſtrings, and tunes the ſaid Inſtruments, in the beſt and neateſt manner. Any Gentlemen and ladies that will honour him with their cuſtom, ſhall be punctually waited upon. He lives at Mr. Gavin Brown's Watch-maker North-ſide of K I N G. STREET.

10

in the *Boston Chronicle* of November 14, 1768, Mr. Harris was a newcomer.

As some of the members of the Puritan congregation became more proficient in singing, they naturally drew together and later were assigned special seats. In this way choirs gradually came into existence before the sterner opposing faction realized the transition. Vocal collections increased in number and by the end of the eighteenth century nearly eighty had appeared in New England alone.

But little of the music in these collections was original, though native composers began to appear. The first man of note was the eccentric, one-eyed, snuff-taking tanner's apprentice, William Billings. He was born in Boston, October 7, 1746, four years after Handel produced *The Messiah* in Dublin, and ten years before Mozart saw the light in Salzburg. Billings' first book, *The New England Psalm Singer*, appeared in the year of Beethoven's birth, 1770. Thus, one hundred and forty years after the founding of Boston, the first book of native music was issued, and with it the publishing of American composition may be said to begin.*It contained one hundred and eight pages and presented one hundred and twenty tunes, and several anthems, as well as twenty-two pages of elementary instruction, and an essay on the nature and properties of musical sound. In 1778 Billings published

---

*James Lyon's Collection of Psalm-tunes, anthems, and hymns entitled *Urania* appeared in Philadelphia in 1761 or 1762. It was based on English sources but of its forty tunes six were by Lyon himself.

a revision and abridgment of his first book entitled *The Singing Mafter's Affistant,* which soon became known as "Billings Best." In his naïve preface to the new book, Billings characterizes his first book as "this infant production of my own Numb-Skull," and further on says, "I have difcovered that many of the pieces in that Book were never worth my printing, or your infpection."

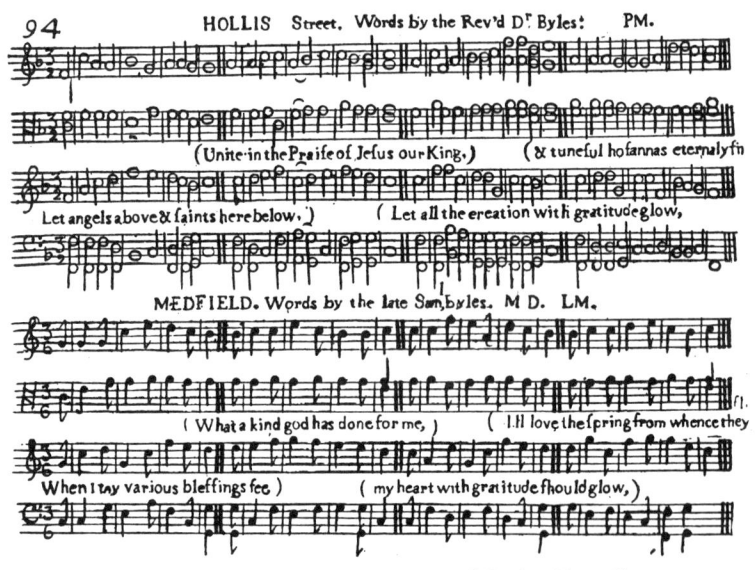

Page from Billings' "New England Psalm Singer"

Billings' music with all its uncouthness was, in comparison with the prevailing style, melodic, cheerful and rhythmic. In 1779 he issued *Mufic in Miniature,* and two years later, *The Pfalm-Singer's Amufement,* which also became popular. His sixth and last book, *The Continental Harmony,* was published in 1794. He died in Boston, September 26, 1800. Billings is said to have been the first to introduce the violoncello in New England churches, as well as the first to use a pitch-pipe to "set the tune." The singing class of forty-eight residents of Stoughton, Massachusetts, he taught in 1774, was formally organized November 7, 1786, shortly after the Revolution, as the Stoughton Musical Society, and still exists.

The fuguing style of Billings' music and its crudities may now provoke a smile, but after a century and a half of the dull and monotonous drawling of a few threadbare psalm tunes the spirited style which Billings introduced must have delighted the young people of his day. He gave to local music a new meaning, a fresh impulse, a greater freedom.

Another notable figure in the musical life of this period was Oliver Holden, born in Shirley, Massachusetts, in 1765. He settled in Charlestown, Massachusetts, in 1788, as a carpenter and joiner and then dropped his tools to become a music teacher. He is remembered to this day by his stirring hymn tune, *Coronation*, which appeared in *The Ameri-*

Holden's Organ and Portrait

can Harmony, published by Holden, in 1792. He prospered and his fine house in Pearl Street, Charlestown, where he wrote *Coronation*, is still standing. The little pipe organ he used is now in the custody of the Bostonian Society in the old State House. In 1797 Holden published *The Worcester Collection of Sacred Harmony*, which had a wide and long continued influence. It was printed from movable types by Isaiah Thomas of Worcester, who advertised in the Boston *Independent Chronicle* of January 26, 1785, that he "has received from England a beautiful fet of mufic types whereby he is enabled to print any kind of Church or other mufic in a neat and elegant manner, cheaper than heretofore done from copper and pewter plates. Specimens to be seen at Battelle's Bofton Book Store, State Street." (See page 22.)

In the latter half of the eighteenth century, because of the victory of choirs and singing schools over "the old way," books of music appeared in profusion. The secular spirit is most manifest in *The Columbian Songfter and Free Mafon's Pocket Companion*, published by E. Larkin, No. 47 Cornhill, Boston, in 1798. "A collection of the neweft and moft celebrated Sentimental, Convivial, Humorous, Satirical, Paftoral, Hunting, Sea and Mafonic fongs, being the largeft and beft collection ever published in America."

∴

While psalmody was predominant in the early musical life of Boston it must not be thought that music for recreation and entertainment had no place, for the first half of the eighteenth century brought to Boston men of rank in the British Navy and Army who were accustomed to the life of English and Continental society. Moreover the various military expeditions to Canada against the French gave New England a taste of the roving life of the soldier and sailor. These conditions, together with increasing prosperity, naturally gave rise to a demand for public entertainment.

The first advertisement of a public concert in America thus far discovered, appeared in the weekly *Boston News-Letter* of December 16-23, 1731: "There will be performed a *Concert of Music* on fundry Inftruments at Mr. Pelham's great Room, being the Houfe of the late Doctor Noyes near the Sun Tavern." The next concerts of record are those of November 23 and December 28, 1732, advertised in the *New England Weekly Journal* of November 13 and December 15, as "Conforts of Mufick performed on fundry inftruments at the Concert Room in Wing's Lane near the Town Dock." This was a room in the George Tavern on what is now Elm Street. The generosity of Peter Faneuil in giving the town Faneuil Hall, finished in 1742, furnished a room in 1744 for a vocal and instrumental concert. Ten years later, Gilbert Deblois, organist of King's Chapel, and his brother built a brick building on the east corner of Hanover and Court Streets. Their shop, the sign of the *Crown and Comb*, was on the ground floor. Above was a hall fitted in a handsome manner for concerts. This was known as "Concert Hall" and for nearly a century was the resort of Bostonians on pleasure bent. It was torn down in 1869 when Hanover Street was widened. The *Boſton Chronicle*, in November, 1768, advertises concerts at the "Muſic-Hall in Brattle Street, oppoſite Dr. Cooper's Meeting-Houſe."

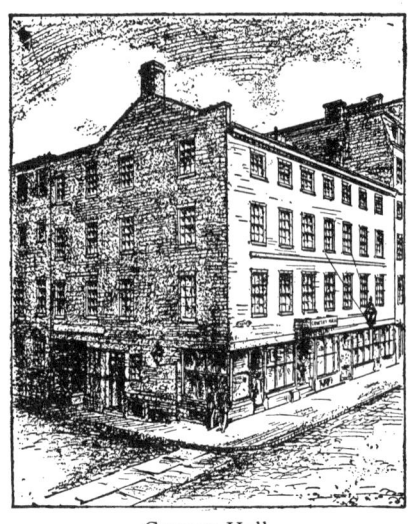

Concert Hall

Concerts at this period were advertised to begin at six o'clock, and the tickets were usually half a dollar or "two shillings—lawful money." At a concert of sacred music performed at the Stone Chapel (King's Chapel), December 11, 1789, under the direction of Mr. William Selby, the chapel's organist, the choruses were by "The Independent Musical Society, the instrumental parts by a Society of Gentlemen, with the band of His Most Christian Majesty's Fleet." This William Selby, harpsichordist, organist, composer, music teacher, active concert manager, and during the stringency of the Revolution a grocer, was one of the chief figures in Boston's musical life between 1772 and his death in December, 1798.

Most of the early concerts seem to have been for

the benefit of the poor of the town and were given by permission of the Selectmen. The name of Handel began to appear in 1770 and occurs not infrequently as "the late celebrated Mr. Handel." The French Revolution drove a number of musicians to the colonies, and after 1793 programs in Boston were in consequence lighter in character.

Although music in the churches had advanced greatly during the century a sidelight is thrown upon it by a writer in the *American Apollo* of April 20, 1792. In "Lines written, rather out of temper, on a Pannel in one of the Pews of S——m Church," he says:

"Could poor King David but for once
To S——m Church repair,
And hear his Pſalms thus warbled out,
Good Lord, how he would ſwear!"

During the last quarter of the century music teachers began to appear and instrumental music to find a place in the home. A French visitor, Brissot de Warville, writing in 1788 regarding Bostonians says: "Music, which their teachers formerly proscribed as a diabolical art, begins to make part of their education. In some houses you hear the forte-piano. This art, it is true, is still in its infancy."

The NEW and FAVOURITE
LIBERTY SONG,
In FREEDOM we're Born. &c.
Neatly engraved on COPPER-PLATE, the
ſize of half a ſheet of Paper,
Set to MUSIC for the VOICE,
And to which is alſo added,
A SET of NOTES adapted to the
GERMAN FLUTE and VIOLIN,
Is juſt publiſhed and to be SOLD at the
LONDON Book-ſtore, King-ſtreet, Boſton,
Price SIXPENCE Lawful ſingle, and
FOURSHILLINGS Lawful, the dozen.

17

That as early as 1768 the publication of sheet-music had begun in Boston is shown by the advertisement reproduced on the preceding page from the *Boſton Chronicle* of October 17.

The publication of secular music prior to the Revolution was very slight, the years of war put a stop to even this, and the period of readjustment and struggle for National Government that followed was equally unfavorable. The opening of the first Congress in 1789 marked the turning point, the old order faded out and in this very year secular music publishing took a start in Boston and Philadelphia, while New York became active in 1793.

Much of the secular music issued was patriotic, or echoed passing events, the bulk of it being altogether ephemeral. Naturally much English music was reprinted, chiefly the songs of Hook, Dibdin, Shield, and Storace. Reprints of the music of Haydn, Gluck, Pleyel, Mozart, and Handel were few in number although their names appear with increasing frequency on concert programs.

While Boston was behind Philadelphia and New York in the publication of secular music, in the output of sacred music it greatly exceeded the rest of the country, while the neighboring towns of Dedham, Newburyport, Salem, Northampton, and Worcester added their quota.

It was not until the close of the century that music-shops, under the name of "magazines" or "emporiums," began to appear. One of the first was opened late in 1797 or early in 1798 by *P. A. Von Hagen, sen. & jun.*, at 55 Marlboro Street, and then at 3 Cornhill (Washington Street), where in 1799 they began to publish music. The constant removals of the early music and book-shops and the frequency with which they changed hands suggest a somewhat precarious existence for the pioneers.

SOME EARLY BOOK AND MUSIC SHOPS

In the early days there was neither the population nor the publication to sustain music-shops. Books of psalmody and the few instruction books were as a rule issued to subscribers and distributed by the author or compiler himself, by his printer, or through book-sellers. The latter were the chief purveyors of music and music-books and continued to be so until the close of the eighteenth century. In fact, this combination of book-selling and music-selling carried well over into the first third of the nineteenth century, when it was fre-

State Street in 1801

quently mixed with the sale of umbrellas and parasols, together with even more mundane articles.

The sale of music was not even confined to bookstores, for the *Boston Gazette* of January 12, 1767, advertises that "*Tanfur's Royal Melody Compleat*, the laſt and beſt Edition, may be had at John Perkins's Shop in Union Street. N. B. At the ſame Place may be had a large aſſortment of Paper Hangings for Rooms."

A prominent mid-century book-shop was the *London Book-Store*, located on the north side of King Street (now State Street), across from the old State House. In 1762 it was kept by James Rivington, afterwards a New York publisher, and then by Rivington and Miller. In 1765 it was kept by John Mein, who had been a book-seller in Edinburgh. His circulating library consisted of above 1200 volumes "in most branches of polite literature, arts and sciences." The character of his music stock is shown by the advertisement (part of a full column ad.) reproduced from the *Boston Gazette* of July 17, 1766.

In 1769 Mein was mobbed for his utterances in favor of the British Government in

April Magazines,
1s lawful each, juſt arrived in the LYDIA, Captain SCOT, to be had of

John Mein,
At the London Book Store, King-ſtreet, Boſton ;

Williams's Univerſal Pſalmodiſt, *a new Edition carefully corrected and improved, with an Addition of near 40 new Tunes and Anthems that have met with univerſal Approbation among the muſical Societies.*

Knapps new Set of Pſalms and Anthems, *with a Paſtoral Hymn by the famous Mr. Addiſon*

Arnold's Complete Pſalmodiſt, or Pſalm ſinger's Companion.

—— Church Muſic reformed
—— Leiceſterſhire Harmony
Green's Body of Pſalmody

his paper the *Bofton Chronicle*, and his failure two years later gave young Henry Knox his opportunity, for he opened a new *London Book-Store* on Cornhill (Washington Street), where the office of the *Boston Globe* now stands. Knox was popular, and his shop became a great resort for British officers and Tory ladies. When the loyal Knox left town at the outbreak of the Revolution in April, 1775, to attain renown as a General and later as Secretary of War, his store was robbed, pillaged of its stock by the Royalists and his business as a bookseller ended.

During the war, business was dislocated, foreign importation of books and music was suspended and bookselling was reduced to the small output of a few printers of American books.

After the war, in 1783, Colonel Ebenezer Battelle, a native of Dedham, opened at No. 8 State Street (no longer King Street) the *Bofton Book-Store*. His music stock is indicated in the advertisement reproduced here from the *Maffachufetts Centinel* of November 6, 1784.

> M U S I C K.
> Lately received, and SOLD at
> E. BATTELLE's Book-Store;.
> STATE-STREET,
> A VALUABLE Collection of MUSICK BOOKS, confifting of Airs, Songs, Country-Dances, Minuets and Marches. —Symphonies, Quartellos, Concertos, Sonatas, Divertilementos, Duettos, Solos, Trios, Oratorios, &c. for the Organ, Harpfichord, Clarinett, French-Horn, Hautboy, Flute, Violin, Violincello, Harp, Piano-Forte, Voice, &c.
> PSALMODY.
> Maffachufetts Harmony.
> Law's elect Harmony.
> ——'s Collection of Hymns,
> ——'s Rules of Pfalmody with Tunes and Chaunts annexed.
> ——'s Select tunes.
> N. B. Books and Stationary as ufual.

Colonel Battelle was a graduate of Harvard, served during the Revolution in the Massachusetts Militia, was made Captain in 1778, Major in 1780 and Colonel of the Boston Regiment in 1784. His military proclivities interfered with his book business, which did not prove profitable, especially under the depreciation of Continental currency, for $4,000 in bills of credit were worth but $100 in silver. On February 1, 1785, Battelle moved to 10 Marlboro Street, but sold out his music and circulating library at 8 State Street to Benjamin Guild. In 1788, as a pioneer member of the Ohio Company, he settled at Marietta, and died in Newport, Ohio, in 1815.

In the *Independent Chronicle* of December 1, 1785, Guild advertises his latest importations.

The following year Guild moved his bookstore to 59 Cornhill, "Firſt door South of the Old-Brick Meeting-Houſe," according to his advertisements in October, 1786.

After Guild's death, in 1792, his administrator, William Pinson Blake, continued the business at 59 Cornhill, being succeeded in 1796 by William Pelham, at the same location where

Imported, in the laſt veſſel from London,
AND NOW SELLING, by
Benjamin Guild,
At the BOSTON BOOK-STORE,
No. 8, STATE-STREET,

GUTHRIE'S Geographical Grammar, publiſhed laſt May, with large additions and improvements, Elegant Extracts, new edition, Buchan's Family Phyſician, new edition, Pulpit and family folio Bibles, with notes and cuts, Peregrine Pickle, Triſtram Shandy, Sentimental Journey; Tom Jones, Gill Blas, Churchill's Poems, Goldſmith's Eſſays, Swift's Polite Converſation, Thomſon's Seaſons, Gay's Fables, Hudibras, Shenſtone's Poetical Works, Moore's Fables, Roderick Random, Joſeph Andrews, Paradiſe Loſt.

Alſo, may be had, (beſides a general aſſortment of books)
The Maſſachuſetts Regiſter; Thomas's, Bickerſtaff's, George's, Low's and Weatherwiſe's Almanacks, for 1786; a large and elegant aſſortment of Account and other Blank-Books; Alphabets; Viſiting Cards; Ink and Ink-Powder; Ink-Stands; Pencils; counting-houſe and other Penknives; Slates; caſes of Surveying Inſtruments; ivory Folders; Spy-Glaſſes; Money-Scales; pocket-Books, Maps; Chairs; and a great variety of other articles.

☞ A few patent LAMPS.

his relative, William Price, previously lived and had a book-store.

William Pelham, born in Williamsburg, Virginia, in 1759, was a grandson of the Peter Pelham who married Mary Copley, mother of the painter, John Singleton Copley. The building at 59 Cornhill (now 219 Washington Street), the original site of Thompson's Spa of today, had been purchased in 1736 by William Price, who published in 1743 his *View of Boston*. Price also dealt in music, for in 1769 he advertises on his map of Boston, "Flutes, Hautboys & Violins, Strings, Muſical Books, Songs, &c."

In the *Independent Chronicle* of October 22, 1804, Pelham makes the following announcement:

William Blagrove was a son of Pelham's sister, Sarah Pelham. In 1808 he was at 61 Cornhill, and the next year at 3 School Street. On December 19, 1810, he advertises in the *Columbian Centinel* the sale of Loo counters, playing cards, chess men, 50 gallons of black sand, and books, including 500 *Blairs Grave* in sheets, and 200 *Curfew*, a play in sheets. The music advertised was "A lot of music, consisting of Songs, Marches, Sonatas, etc. (a Catalogue of which may be seen), amounting to $400 or upwards, will be sold in sums of 10 dollars at 25 per

W. PELHAM,
RESPECTFULLY appriſes his friends and cuſtomers of the Removal of his
CIRCULATING LIBRARY,
from No. 59, Cornhill, to No. 5, School-Street.
W. P. having placed this branch of his buſineſs entirely under the direction of Mr. WILLIAM BLAGROVE, ſolicits a continuance of thoſe favors he has been accuſtomed to receive during eight years paſt, the greater part of which time he has been conſtantly aſſiſted by Mr. Blagrove, whoſe habitual attention to the wiſhes of his Cuſtomers precludes the neceſſity of recommendation.——A new Catalogue containing all the late additions, is in forwardneſs, and will ſhortly be publiſhed.
☞ BOOKS and STATIONARY for Sale, as uſual, at No. 59, CORNHILL.   Oct. 22.

cent discount, in sums of 50 to 100 dollars at 33 per cent discount from the retail price."

On April 27, 1811, this notice appeared in the *Columbian Centinel:*

Samuel Hale Parker was born in Wolfboro, N. H., in 1781, the son of Matthew Stanley Gibson Parker. His uncles were Judge William Parker and Sheriff John Parker of New Hampshire, and Bishop Samuel Parker of Boston. His brothers were Matthew Stanley Parker, cashier of the Suffolk Bank, and William Sewall Parker, a book-seller of Troy, N.Y.

> Union Circulating Library,
> *No. 3, School-street.*
> SAMUEL H. PARKER, respectfully informs the patrons of this establishment and the public, that he has undertaken the future management of the business (Mr. BLAGROVE having relinquished it) and solicits continuance of the distinguished patronage it has hitherto experienced. Constant attention will be paid to the wishes of his customers, and large ADDITIONS are contemplated to be made during the summer, to the stock of circulating books. apr 27
>
> NOTICE.
> W. BLAGROVE having relinquished the management of the business of the *Union Circulating Library*, respectfully calls upon those of his late customers from whom small arrearages are still due, for immediate settlement, as he is about closing his accounts with the Proprietor of the Establishment.
> ***Books which have been detained *over one month* must be returned; and all detained over 6 weeks will be considered as purchased, according to the conditions, unless immediately sent home. apr 27

After serving an apprenticeship to a book-binder in 1802, Samuel H. Parker began as a book-binder on Court Street, continuing that business until he took over the shop of William Blagrove in 1811. This shop was on the south side of School Street, three doors from Marlboro (now Washington Street). He continued at 3 School Street until he moved to 4 Cornhill, where he temporarily joined his interests with the book-sellers, Munroe & Francis, under the name *Munroe, Francis and Parker*, who so advertise in the *Columbian Centinel* of September 13, 1815. The *Centinel* of December 23, 1815, advertising the first concert of the Handel and Haydn Society states: "Tickets of admission may be obtained at the Bookstores of Munroe, Francis and Parker," and others, including "G. Graupner, Franklin Street." In 1816 Parker withdrew from the firm but remained at the corner of Water Street and Cornhill.

View from Pemberton Hill in 1816, from the painting by Salmon

From time to time Parker advertises various book publications, and October 18, 1817, he announces in the *Columbian Centinel:* "Three Sacred Songs by Moore delightfully set to music by Oliver Shaw of Providence and sung by him at late Oratorios. *This World is all a Fleeting Show*, *Mary's Tears*, and *Thou art, O God! the Life and Light*, for sale at Parker's Circulating Library, 4 Cornhill." The same advertisement tells the public that he has "Just received a fresh supply of Vancouver's Iron Cement for mending glass and crockery."

The next year, 1818, his circulating library and music store were moved to 12 Cornhill, one door south of the shop formerly occupied by Henry Knox. Here, in 1822, he advertises his "just published" edition of the Waverley Novels. Concerts of the period advertise "Tickets to be had at Mr. Parker's Music Store, No. 12 Cornhill, and at Mr. Graupner's Music Store, Franklin Street." In 1825 Parker moved to 164 Washington Street, between Milk and Franklin, where he remained until fire destroyed the premises.

In the *Boston Transcript* of November 1, 1833, the following item appeared: "Fire. About half past 3 o'clock this morning fire was discovered in the cellar of building No. 164 Washington Street, owned by Mr. Benj. Guild; insured for $7,500. The lower floor was occupied by Mr. Samuel H. Parker for a library and music store, and John Price, optician. The 2d story was occupied by Mr. Benj. Bradley, bookbinder, and Mr. Chas. Bradlee, music publisher, and the upper stories by Mr. Parker as a printing office. Mr. Parker was insured for $10,000 in book stock and $3,000 on printing stock. A large portion of his library was destroyed, together with two valuable pianos, two printing presses, and a large amount in sheet stock. We are happy to learn, however, that none of the valuable stereotype plates of the Waverley Novels were lost, excepting one or two works which were in the process of being printed. The residue were stored in another place. Still his loss is severe, and just at the time he was upon the point of realizing the fruit of eight or ten years' hard labor in completing his edition of Scott's Novels, which would have been finished and come to market in December. Mr. Chas. Bradlee lost a large portion of his sheet music and plates."

In the *Transcript* of January 4, 1834, Parker advertises "Piano-fortes just received and for sale," at 10 School Street, but in the issue of April 5 "Sam'l H. Parker informs his friends that he has taken half of the store occupied by Mr. L. C. Bowles, 141 Washington Street, where he will renew the sale of *Music* and publishing the Waverley Novels which have been so unfortunately discontinued by the loss of his stock at the late fire," etc., etc. This location was three doors south of School Street. On July 1 he advertises that "He will have for sale all the Music published by Mr. C. Bradlee, with a constant supply of the new and fashionable Songs and Piano-forte pieces published at the South."

Parker's store became more and more a musical centre, and on December 11, 1834, the *Transcript* states that "S. H. Parker has removed his music store from 141 to 107 Washington Street." This shop, on the south corner of Williams Court, was shortly after occupied in part by the music store of Oliver Ditson, who had some eight years earlier been in his employ.

At about the same time (January 20, 1835) the building into which Parker had moved was purchased by James A. Dickson who, as an actor, had come from

England in 1796 to appear at the opening of the Haymarket Theatre. Later he was manager of the Boston Theatre on Federal Street up to 1820, when he opened a "music saloon" on Market Street (now Cornhill), which had been recently made a thoroughfare. He was located there at the corner of Franklin Avenue for twenty years, but about 1835 Dickson turned his activities more and more from selling music to marketing Day and Martin's blacking and Crosse and Blackwell's jam.

THE NINETEENTH CENTURY

State House and Common about 1820

IN 1800 Boston was a town of about 25,000 inhabitants, the earlier provincialism was passing, and evidences of interest in music for its own sake were becoming manifest. Music teachers had been increasing in numbers since the close of the Revolution, while growing prosperity and population gradually made it possible for shops for the sale of music and musical instruments to exist without the aid of other commodities. The change, however, was slow and the venturesome pioneers were as a rule musicians of standing in the community. Such was Gottlieb Graupner who, about 1800, began to publish music. This he engraved and printed with his own hands and sold at his "Musical Academy," No. 6 Franklin Street,

Gottlieb Graupner

where he also sold pianos and other instruments until February, 1820. According to *The Euterpiad*, his talented wife, Catherine, was "for many years the only female vocalist in Boston." She died in 1821, and Graupner in 1836.

Graupner was an all-round musician, at home on many instruments, and thirty years of age when, in 1797, he settled in Boston, where from 1798 until 1815 he was "the musical oracle." In 1810 the few instrumentalists of professional experience then living in Boston, together with a few amateurs, were organized by Graupner into The Philharmonic Society.* He had been oboist in Haydn's orchestra in London in 1791-1792, and soon his little orchestra practiced Haydn's symphonies for its own gratification and gave concerts of which that on November 24, 1824, was the last.

Graupner's pioneer work helped to prepare the way for larger things. The publisher in a national sense was yet to come, and there is little doubt that Graupner influenced his early career.

Oliver Ditson was of a family of Scotch descent living in Billerica, Massachusetts, in the last years of the seventeenth century. His grandfather, Samuel Ditson, was a Revolutionary soldier, living in Burlington, Massachusetts. Oliver's father, Joseph Ditson, born there in 1772, married in 1797, Lucy, the daughter of

*This name is also given as *Philharmonio* and *PhiloHarmonic*. A Philharmonic Society existed in 1799, according to a notice in the *Columbian Centinel* of April 6, 1799. Possibly it was the same society.

31

Solomon Pierce of Lexington, who was wounded on the morning of April 19, 1775, and later took part in the battle of Bennington.

Upon his marriage Joseph Ditson came to Boston. At that time property on the north side of Beacon Hill was being developed. Harrison Gray Otis had just finished his house, still standing on the corner of Lynde and Cambridge Streets. The Suffolk Registry of Deeds records that Joseph Ditson purchased of Appleton Prentiss a lot 40 x 70 feet on the newly laid out street between Russell and Irving Streets. Here he built a house in which he lived until 1810 when he moved to 74 Prince Street, near Copp's Hill, where on October 20, 1811, his fifth child, Oliver, was born. This house, now numbered 114, is on the west side of Prince Street.

The year 1811 was notable for the birth of Liszt and Thackeray, Charles Sumner and Harriet Beecher Stowe. The year before Chopin, Schumann, and Ole Bull were born. Of men destined to be significant in Boston's life, Emerson was then a lad of eight attending the public grammar school, Hawthorne was seven years old, Garrison six, Longfellow and Whittier four, and Oliver Wendell Holmes a baby of two. The year following, 1812, saw the outbreak of war with England as well as Napoleon's retreat from Moscow.

On Washington's Birthday, 1815, a musical jubilee was held in King's Chapel to celebrate the Peace of Ghent which concluded the war of 1812. Out of this originated, a few weeks later, The Handel and Haydn Society. One of the organizers and a member of the first board of trustees was Samuel H. Parker, then a member of Trinity choir. Another of the founders was G. Graupner, at whose Music Hall, 6 Franklin Street, the first meetings to organize the Society were held. It gave its first public concert in King's Chapel on Christmas Eve, 1815, and in 1818 gave the first complete performance of an oratorio in this country when it presented *The Messiah*. It was this society that in 1821 (dated 1822) published Lowell Mason's first collection of music after the publishers of Philadelphia and Boston had declined it. This was the very successful *Handel and Haydn Society Collection of Church Music*.

King's Chapel

It was in 1823 that young Oliver Ditson having finished his school life in the Eliot School on North Bennett Street, entered the employ of Colonel Parker, then at 12 Cornhill (Washington Street).

In 1824 the Public Garden was created on what had been an unsightly batch of mud on the west side of Charles Street. Boston was at this time a veritable garden city, and Summer Street with its overshadowing trees, lovely gardens and fine mansions, well merited its name.

In 1826 Lowell Mason settled in Boston, was next year made president and conductor of The Handel and Haydn Society, and thus began his notable public career not only as "The Father of American church music," but as the pioneer in inaugurating and developing the teaching of music in the public schools, formally introduced in 1838 as a regular branch of study in the Boston schools after two years of experimental work by Mason and his associate, Wm. C. Woodbridge.

In was in 1826 that young Ditson left S. H. Parker to apprentice himself to Isaac R. Butts, then printing *The North American Review*. Later he was with Alfred Mudge, and while there had charge of the printing for Colonel Parker, his former employer. At this time Ditson lived at 10 Province House Court, across the way from the prominent musician, Gottlieb Graupner, who then lived at No. 1. His son, John Henry Howard Graupner, and Oliver Ditson had been boys together, and the daughter of the former records the fact that her father carried for life a scar resulting from a wound given him by Oliver in some boyish rough and tumble play.

Mr. Ditson's innate fondness for music, his three years' training with Colonel Parker in the book and music business, his seven years' training as a printer, and possibly, also, his friendly relationship with the Graupner family, led him in 1835 to start in the music business at 107 Washington Street, just south of Williams Court.

He was at this time organist and choirmaster of the Bulfinch Street Church. The *Transcript* of October 13, 1834, advertises "SACRED CONCERT. The Singing Choir attached to Rev. Mr. Deane's Church in Bulfinch Street will perform a Concert of Sacred Music on Sunday Evening next, Oct. 19th at 6 1-2 o'clock. Tickets at 25 cents each, may be procured at S. H. Parker's Music Store, 141 Washington st; J. M. Smith's, Druggist, corner of School and Tremont sts.; and at the door on the evening of performance. Oliver Ditson, Sec'ry."

In December, 1834, as mentioned above, Colonel Parker moved from 141 Washington Street to No. 107. This brought him and his former employee together again under the same roof. Boston's population was then about 75,000. Postal rates were high, for it cost 18 3-4 cents to send a letter of a single sheet from Boston to New York. These were the days of the stage-coach, although they were soon to decline through the advent of railroads. It is recorded that in 1832 there were ninety-three stage lines running out of Boston.

What is, perhaps, the first mention of Oliver Ditson as a publisher appears in the *Saturday Evening Gazette* of June 6, 1835, which states in a reading notice: "Mr. Oliver Ditson has just published a new song entitled *There's not a Leaf within the Bower*. It was composed by F. Valentine, and arranged as a duet by Ch. Zeuner. It is for sale at Parker's Music Store." This was copyrighted June 5th by Oliver Ditson. The *Transcript* of June 20, 1835 says: "Ditson has in press *The City Guards Quick-step*, composed by Walsh, and arranged as a duett for two flutes by Zeuner," and on July 9th advertises the same number as "Just published and for sale by S. H. Parker." This number was also copyrighted in the name of Oliver Ditson.

The *Gazette* of November 14, 1835, advertises a concert of the Handel and Haydn Society—"Tickets at Oliver Ditson's," and the *Transcript* of December 22, 1835, advertises a performance of *The Messiah* by the same society—"Tickets at Ditson's Music Store." The same paper in its issue of March 30, 1836, advertises the *Oratorio of David*, just published, as for sale at "Ditson's Music Store, 107 Washington Street," and that tickets for its approaching performance by the Handel and Haydn Society are to be had "at the Music Store of O. Ditson." Tickets for a concert by the Boston Academy were advertised in the *Boston Courier* of April 3d, "for sale at O. Ditson's."

On April 6th, the song, *My Heart's in the Highlands*, is advertised in the *Transcript* as for sale at "Ditson's Music Store." Apparently the younger man, by his energy and enthusiasm, was gaining precedence over his senior, who solved the problem by making

Oliver his partner. The *Transcript* of April 5, 1836, contained the notice of copartnership.

The growing business of the new firm led them to seek better quarters and in 1838 they had the good fortune to locate in the old gambrel-roofed building that since 1712 had stood on the site of the home of Anne Hutchinson, the first woman champion of intellectual freedom in America. In this old shop at the corner of Washington and School Streets books were sold continuously from 1828 to July, 1903. In 1837 the bookseller was Wm. D. Ticknor, but it was in the days of James T. Fields that *The Old Corner Bookstore* became a gathering place for "the New England circle which compelled the world to acknowledge that there was an American literature."

> COPARTNERSHIP NOTICE. S. H. PARKER, having associated MR OLIVER DITSON with him in the Music and Piano Forte business, that department will be conducted at 107 Washington street, in future, under the firm of PARKER & DITSON—who have now on hand a large collection of Music, and are constantly publishing and receiving from the other publishers in the United States, the fashionable and popular Music of the time.
> SAMUEL H. PARKER,
> OLIVER DITSON.
> Boston, April 5, 1836.
> S. H. P continues to publish the Waverly Novels, as usual, from his stereotyped edition, and orders will be received for them at the above store, either in wholesale numbers from the trade, or by single copy, folded or bound.
> is3t   april 5

> **PARKER & DITSON,**
> DEALERS IN
> **Piano Fortes & Sheet Music,**
> 107 *Washington Street, Boston.*
> sept 30   is6m

> TO THE MUSICAL PUBLIC.
> REMOVAL. PARKER & DITSON, Dealers in Piano Fortes and Sheet Music, have removed to 135 Washington st, corner of School st, where may be found all the fashionable Music of the day.
> N. B.—Connected with the store, P. & D. have an extensive Wareroom for the sale of new and second hand Piano Fortes. Pianos to let.   is4t   may 5

The Old Corner Bookstore

This location was then No. 135 Washington Street.

37

In 1840 Mr. Ditson married Miss Catherine Delano, a descendant of William Bradford, second Governor of Plymouth Colony. It was in this year that Boston was chosen as the terminus of the Cunard Line and the first regular trans-Atlantic steamer service began. Railway connection with Worcester, Lowell and Providence had been made in 1835, but with Albany not until 1841. There was not then a telegraph line in the world; Boston had a population of 93,383, New York 312,710, Philadelphia 93,665; Chicago was a frontier village of 4479, while Kansas City, St. Paul, Minneapolis and San Francisco had not been heard of.

Intersection of the Providence and Worcester railroads, 1838

It was just at this time that Henry Russell, the English ballad singer, visited Boston, and his songs, *The Ship on Fire*, *The Maniac*, *The Gambler's Wife*, and others, were being sung with fervor in drawing rooms; while, on the other hand, Margaret Fuller was holding her famous "Conversations" at Miss Peabody's rooms on

(No. 135)   West side of Washington Street in 1845   (No. 107)

West Street, and the Transcendentalists were making their Brook Farm experiment, with John S. Dwight as teacher of music and Latin.

In 1842 Mr. Ditson acquired the interests of his senior partner as appears in the Dissolution of Copartnership notice, dated March 17, and printed in the *Transcript* the same day.

In need of larger quarters, Oliver Ditson moved in 1844 from the Old Corner Bookstore to a neighbor-

No. 115 to No. 107 Washington Street in 1845

39

ing location at 115 Washington Street, four doors south of Williams Court. In the previous view of the west side of Washington Street the building at the right is No. 107, where Parker and Ditson were first located; the building at the left is No. 135, the Old Corner Bookstore location; while the sign to the right of the lamp post is that of Oliver Ditson at No. 115. In 1845 Mr. Ditson took into his employ a lad of fifteen, John C. Haynes, at the weekly stipend of $1.50. Eight years later, in 1853, the value of the young man was recognized by giving him an interest in the business, and on January 1, 1857, he was admitted to copartnership and the house name changed to Oliver Ditson & Co. In this year Mr. Ditson erected for his firm a building at 277, now 451 Washington Street.

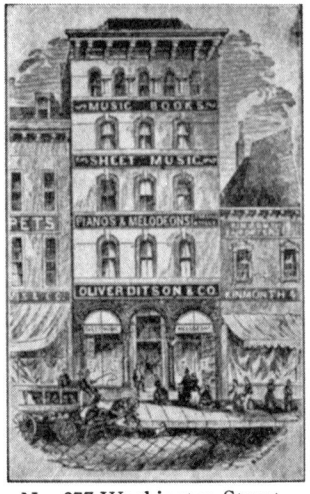

No. 277 Washington Street

It should be noted that Oliver Ditson's early friend and neighbor, John Henry Howard Graupner, had charge of his music printing and engraving department from 1850, or earlier, until 1880. He was a good pianist and trained musician and son of the pioneer, Gottlieb Graupner, who taught him music engraving.

∴

The year 1841 is notable in that Beethoven's symphonies the *First* and *Fifth* were then first heard in Boston. They were performed by the Academy of Music Orchestra, of from twenty-five to forty players, which for seven winters gave a series of six to eight concerts, the last in the spring of 1847. It was at one of its concerts, March 7, 1846, that Wm. Mason, then seventeen, made his first appearance as a pianist.

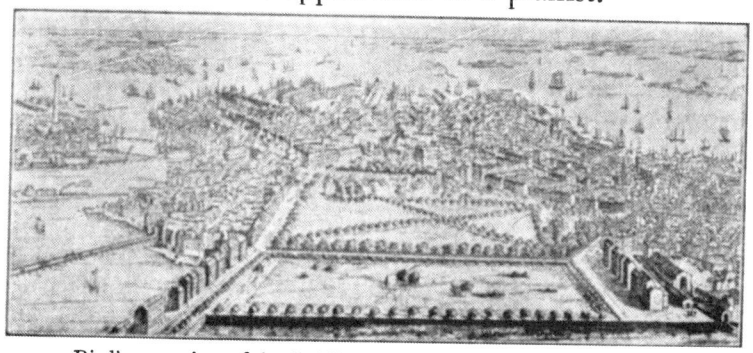

Bird's-eye view of the Public Garden and Common, about 1850

These concerts were succeeded by those of the Musical Fund Society, which for eight seasons gave orchestral concerts in the old Tremont Temple, its last concert being given April, 1855, in the then new Boston Music Hall.

A still better organization, rich in soloists, was the Germania Orchestra, which from 1848 to 1854, travelled, but gave from eighty to ninety of its concerts in Boston, where they made their first appearance April 14, 1849, and gave twenty-two concerts in six weeks. This little orchestra of twenty-three was sometimes doubled by the addition of local musicians. The precision, delicacy and beauty of their performances of the best music left a lasting influence.

It was this orchestra that brought Carl Zerrahn to Boston as its first flute. In 1854 he became conductor of the Handel and Haydn Society, and in 1855 he organized the Philharmonic Orchestra, which gave regular concerts until 1863. In 1865 Zerrahn was made conductor of the orchestra of the Harvard Musical Association, which for seventeen years maintained symphony concerts of a high standard.

Carl Zerrahn

In the musical life of America for many years no single man wielded so potent an influence for musical righteousness as Theodore Thomas. He had a whole-souled belief in the power of good music and devoted his life to making it known. The frequent visits of his orchestra to Boston overshadowed the less disciplined and imperfect local body, sharpened musical perception, and wakened concert-goers to the need of an orchestra of like technical refinement and masterly leadership. This need was generously met by Mr. Henry Lee Higginson when he founded the Boston Symphony

Henry Lee Higginson

Orchestra, which gave its first concert under Georg Henschel, October 22, 1881, and under Gericke, Nikisch, and their successors, has developed into the present unique organization.

It was the Harvard Musical Association, organized in 1837 by John S. Dwight, Henry K. Oliver, William Wetmore Story, Christopher P. Cranch, and others, that by its regular *soirées* from 1844 to 1850 initiated Boston into the beauties of chamber music. Stimulated by these affairs the Mendelssohn Quintette Club was organized with Thomas Ryan as its leading spirit. It was the first chamber music organization of its type in the country and gave its first concert December 14, 1849. For nearly fifty years this club travelled over the United States, making classical music known to multitudes for the first time.

It was also the moral backing of the Harvard Musical Association that led John S. Dwight to establish *Dwight's Journal of Music* in 1852. For six years he was editor, publisher, and proprietor, when, in 1858, the magazine was taken over by Oliver Ditson & Co., who published it until the end of 1878, Mr. Dwight continuing as editor. It was carried on by other publishers until 1881, when it

John S. Dwight

ceased to exist. Its first number was issued April 10, 1852; its last, September 3, 1881. This pioneer magazine was a notable factor in moulding musical opinion and its pages are the history of music in the United States during the twenty-nine years of its existence.

Giulia Grisi

Jenny Lind in 1850

While foreign artists had come and gone, the year 1850 ushered in a notable galaxy, beginning with Jenny Lind and her memorable concerts, the lovely Sontag, and the great Alboni, followed by Patti, Grisi and Mario, Adelaide Phillips, Brignoli, Parepa Rosa, and a host of lesser singers.

It was in February, 1853, that Jenny Lind was married to Otto Goldschmidt, her accompanist, in the house in quaint Louisburg Square, at the left in the illustration. It stands

44

Urso at 11

Teresa Carreño, Anna Mehlig, Rubinstein, von Bülow, Essipoff, and others.

Of violinists, Vieuxtemps, Ole Bull, Sivori, and Camilla Urso, "the girl violinist," were early comers, followed

Carreño at 10

almost on the site of the apple orchard of Boston's first inhabitant.

Of pianists, Thalberg, who came in 1857, was perhaps the first of great rank. The early sixties brought home from Europe, Gottschalk; then came the war and a lull, followed by the girl wonder,

Great Organ in Music Hall

by Wieniawski, Wilhelmj, Remenyi, Sauret, and others.

Organ playing in the country was given a stimulus when the great organ in Boston Music Hall was opened November 2, 1863. This large instrument was

45

the first thorough concert organ in the country. A notable group of organists, B. J. Lang, John K. Paine, Eugene Thayer, S. P. Tuckerman, John H. Wilcox, and George W. Morgan were the first to play upon it.

B. J. Lang

The sensational event of 1869 was the monster Peace Jubilee, organized by P. S. Gilmore; Carl Zerrahn was general director; John K. Paine and Dudley Buck conducted compositions of their own; Julius Eichberg wrote for the occasion his *To Thee, O Country*, now sung in the schools everywhere, and Ole Bull and Carl Rosa played in the big orchestra, while Parepa Rosa and Adelaide Phillips were the chief singers. A festival building large enough to seat thirty thousand persons was erected near the site of the present Copley Plaza Hotel; the orchestra numbered one thousand, and the chorus ten thousand. The sensitive John S. Dwight refused to endorse the Jubilee in his *Journal of Music* and fled to Nahant to escape the cannons, anvils, bells, big organ, eighty-four trombones, eighty-three tubas, as many cornets, and

Julius Eichberg

seventy-five drums, which with three hundred and thirty strings and one hundred and nineteen wood-wind, made "an ensemble of fearful and wonderful sonority."

The ambitious Gilmore found another opportunity at the close of the Franco-Prussian War when he organized on a still larger scale the International Peace Jubilee of June, 1872. This time the auditorium seated fifty thousand; the chorus, collected from over the country as far west as Omaha, numbered twenty thousand and the orchestra two thousand. Johann Strauss and Franz Abt led their own compositions. Mme. Rudersdorff was the chief singer, and famous bands from London, Dublin, Paris, Berlin, Washington, and New York were features. Though the first Jubilee cost $283,000, it left a balance of nearly $10,000 in the treasury; the second "colossal musical picnic" left a deficit of $100,000 to be made up by the guarantors, among them Oliver Ditson.

Hermine Rudersdorff

In contrast to these monster festivals were the smaller and musically more important triennial festivals of the Handel and Haydn Society. It was at the festival of 1871 that about half of Bach's *St. Matthew Passion Music* was given for the first time in America, still more was given in 1874, and on Good Friday, 1879, the entire work had a notable performance in a two-session concert.

How recent serious composition in the larger forms is in America, is indicated by the fact that our pioneer symphonist, John K. Paine, left us as recently as 1906. It was in the year of MacDowell's birth, 1861, that he returned to Cambridge from study in Germany. His first symphony was played in 1876, and when those in charge of the Centennial Exposition sought the two native composers of greatest prominence to write the music for the opening ceremonies they selected John K. Paine and Dudley Buck.

John K. Paine

Since then a notable group have enriched American composition with symphonies, orchestral works, chamber music and choral works, while a host have written in small forms; but to speak of men until recently with us or of the many now active in creative work, interpretation and education, is beyond the scope of this brief sketch of a bygone day.

Dudley Buck

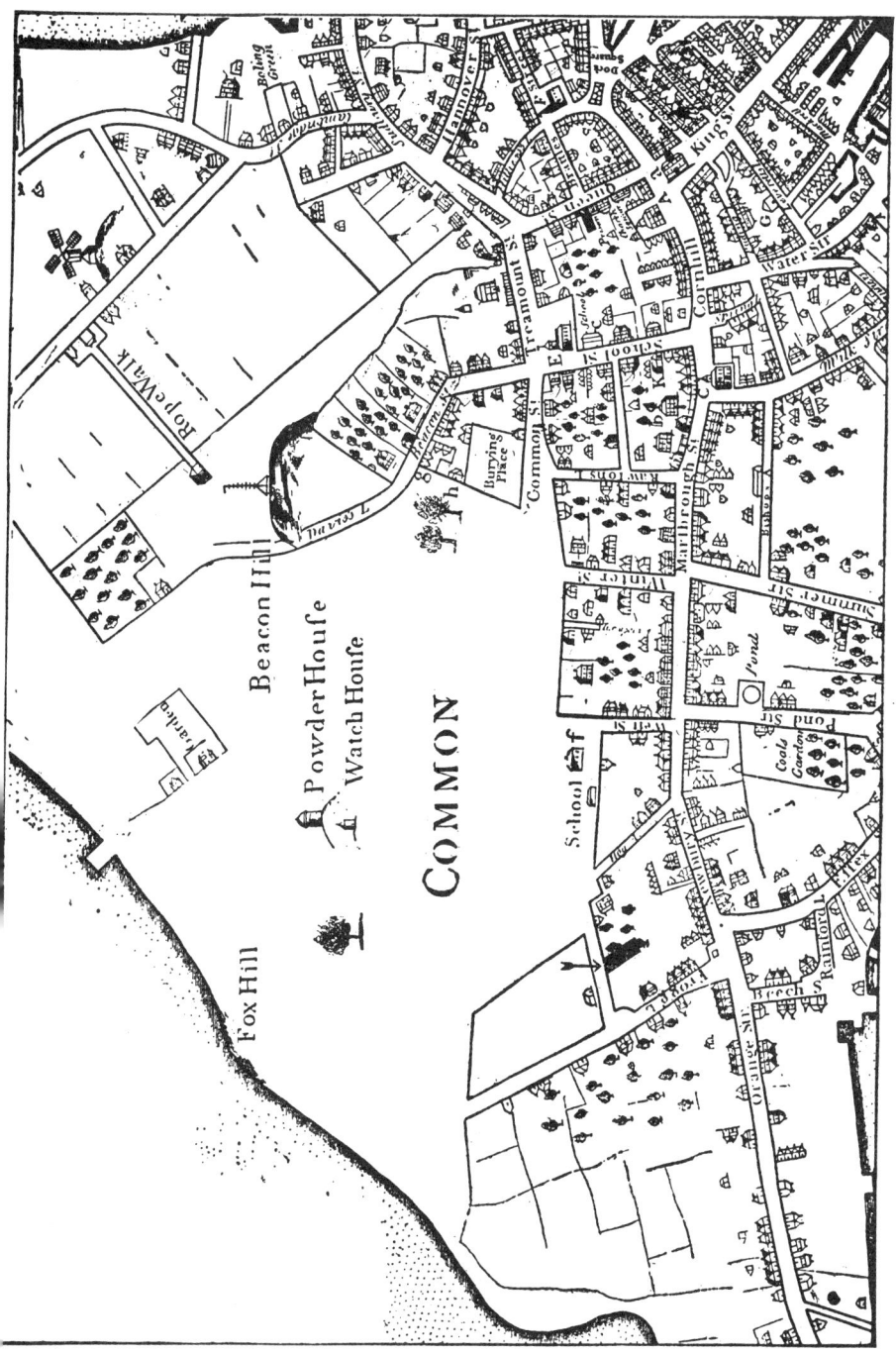

From Bonner's Map of Boston, 1722
(The arrow points to the site of the Hay-Market Theatre)

SITE OF THE HAY-MARKET THEATRE

Common Street from West Street to Frog Lane (Boylston Street) in 1800

Among the most prominent and wealthy citizens of Boston, in its early days as a town, was Henry Webb, a merchant, who came from Salisbury, England, in 1637.

He had an only daughter, Margaret, who, in 1642, married Jacob Sheafe, and on the death of her father in 1660 his large estate of nearly £8000 came to her and her daughters, Elizabeth and Mehitable Sheafe. Her husband, Jacob Sheafe, had died in the previous year, 1659. His tomb in King's Chapel Burial Ground states that "Sheafe ſometime lived in Cranbrook in Kent in Ould England." Sheafe's estate inventoried over £8000. With this double inheritance the widow, wealthy and still young (forty) was married about 1665 to Thomas Thacher, son of Rev. Peter Thacher, rector of St. Edmund's, Salisbury, England. This son was also a minister, first at Weymouth and later, in 1669, he became the first pastor of the Old South Church, Boston.

Mrs. Thacher invested much of her wealth in real

estate, and in 1674 took a mortgage on a house facing the Common from Eneas Salter, a mason. Salter had previously purchased from Martin Saunders and at the time of purchase Salter resided in the house. The house, situated on the lower end of the Common, on its east side, had but a cart path running in front along the unfenced Common used for the pasturing of the cattle of the freemen of the town. On the north side of the lot this path, known today as Mason Street, branched off and led to a lane running eastward to the high-road. The pasturage of cows on the Common must have needed restriction at an early date, for on May 18, 1646, "It is ordered, y^t ther shalbe kept on the Common bye ye Inhabitants of ye towne but 70 milch kine." "It is ordered, y^t if any defire to kep fheep, hee may kep foure fheep in liew of a cow."

Rev. Thomas Thacher died in 1678 and his widow Margaret, in 1694. In 1697 a partition of her property was made between her two daughters by her first husband, Jacob Sheafe: Elizabeth, who married Jonathan Corwin, and Mehitable, who married her second cousin, Sampson Sheafe, of London. He came to Boston about 1670, marrying Mehitable about 1673. The young people resided in the house on the Common at the time of the partition, but a few years later Sampson Sheafe was made deputy collector of customs and went to Newcastle, New Hampshire, to reside. They had several children born in Boston, one of them was Jacob Sheafe, born in 1682. The map of 1722 and the illustrations show how lonely the Common must have been even at a much later date. It is not surprising, therefore, to read in the diary of Mr. Lawrence Hammond, June 9, 1688: "This Evening Mr. Sampſon Sheafe was ſet upon in Boſton Common & knockt downe & robbed by two Ruffins, One Humbleton being preſent, who it is judged, hyred them to do it." On returning to Boston Sampson Sheafe held the office of clerk in the Inferior Court of Common Pleas and died in Boston in 1726. In 1728, the year when the first row of trees was planted along the Common, his widow, Mehitable Sheafe, transferred to her son Jacob the house on the Common, he to pay her £50 a year during her life. In 1712 Jacob Sheafe had been approved by the selectmen to teach the school in Queen Street which stood where the exit from the East Boston Tunnel was located a few years ago. Later he taught the school on the Common near his father's house. Proficient with his quill pen as were schoolmasters in those days he was called *ſcrivener* as well as schoolmaster. When the day's work was done the young schoolmaster could in a few moments reach the water's edge at the foot of the Common, where, according to Justice Sewall's diary, there was a beach which was the favorite landing place for persons coming by boat from Roxbury or Cambridge. Under date of July 6, 1720, he wrote: "Rode to Commencem[t] . . . Had a pleaſant paſſage home by water with Mr. Wendell and his Family. Landed at the bottom of the Common."

On the death of his father, young Jacob improved the brew house which stood in the southeast portion of the land, back of his house. The frontage of his land on the Common was one hundred and thirty-seven feet; the lot had a depth of one hundred and forty-nine feet. He was also a collector of taxes from 1738 to 1746. On February 23, 1744, a fire broke out on his premises which the *Boston Evening-Post* of Monday the 27th reports as follows:

"Laſt Thurſday, between two and three o'Clock in the Afternoon, a Fire broke out in Mr. *Sheafe's* Malt-Houſe near the Common, which in a very little Time entirely conſumed the ſame, with his Brew-Houſe, and ſeveral other Buildings, alſo all his Stock, (which was very large) and Utenſils; and 'twas with great Difficulty that his Dwelling Houſe was preſerved from the Flames. 'Tis ſaid Mr. *Sheafe's* Loſs is at leaſt *Two Thouſand Pounds*. The Wind blowing exceſſive high at Weſt when the Accident happened, a large Barn full of Hay, and another Building at a conſiderable Diſtance from the Fire, were consumed; and the *White Horſe* Tavern being ſet on Fire, very narrowly eſcaped being deſtroyed."

This loss, with the difficulty of finding a sale for his strong beer, forced Sheafe to petition in 1746 for a license to keep a tavern. His health failing and becoming blind in 1753 he sold the property to Abiah Holbrook, schoolmaster. In 1761 Jacob Sheafe's life ended. During the eighteenth century the recently widened Avery Street was known as Sheafe's Lane, and the White Horse tavern was a little south of its junction with Newbury (Washington) Street.

Holbrook, the writing master, born in Boston in 1718, was son of Abiah Holbrook, a kegmaker by trade, but for many years a member of the town watch and later a sexton and grave digger. The younger Abiah petitioned in 1741 to open a school to teach writing and arithmetic. In 1742 he was chosen usher of Mr. Proctor's North Writing School and in 1743 was made Master of the South Writing School* on the Common where he had more than one hundred and fifty scholars.

In 1744 he opened a school to teach the rules of psalmody. In 1746 he married and lived in the Sheafe house, which he bought in 1753.

*Marked f on the old map of the Common, page 49.

In 1762 and 1763 Abiah Holbrook engaged in the book business quite extensively to judge by his large advertisement in the *Massachusetts Gazette* of July 21, 1763, reproduced in part on the preceding page. It should be noted that music books head his list.

He died in 1769, leaving his estate to his widow during her widowhood and to support his parents during their lives, and then the estate was to be divided among his brothers and sisters. "Aſ to the curious alphabet containing the Ten Commandments and other Scripture pieces wrote in all the hands of Great Britain in ſeveral different colors with neat borders round the ſame which I did only for my amuſement, though ſeven years in compleating them, I reſerve unto my wife to diſpoſe of them to the Curious, for her ſole advantage." At the lowest estimation he put the price at £100 lawful money and desired that John Hancock have the first offer of them to purchaſe for Harvard College "always to remain there to be ſeen by the curious."

Abiah Holbrook, junior, had a younger brother Samuel, born in 1729, who was evidently his pupil, and became a schoolmaster in 1745, and the next year Abiah, whose scholars numbered two hundred and twenty, had him as an assistant.

In 1749 Samuel had a salary of £50 as usher of his brother's school and in 1750 was chosen master of the Writing School in Queen (Court) Street. In 1754 he resigned and opened a private school for writing and arithmetic which he carried on to 1769 when he succeeded his brother Abiah, just deceased, as master of the South Writing School in the Common. Here he continued up to March, 1780, when the school was destroyed by fire and he received burns. His brother's widow having a room in her house (the Sheafe mansion) that would accommodate seventy or eighty scholars the town desired its use but she refused. Samuel Holbrook being in poor health opened a private school near by and boarded some of the scholars.

His health still poor in 1781 "he would wait on Ladies and Gentlemen at their abode, or could be feen at his School in Court Square or his dwelling at New Bofton" (West End). In 1782 he removed his school to opposite the Quaker Meeting House in Congress Street. By this we see he had no benefit from his brother's house after Abiah's death. Abiah's widow by right of dower and by purchase acquired title to the Sheafe-Holbrook house to the great disadvantage of her husband's other heirs. Dying in 1794 she left Abiah's "alphabetical piece of penmanship called Knotwork" to Harvard College where it may still be seen "by the curious." Her executors that year sold the estate to Israel Hatch, stage owner and tavern keeper, who kept the house as a tavern, for which purpose it was used until torn down in the first part of the next century.

Joshua Eaton, of Charlestown, who had been a drummer in Bond's Middlesex Regiment in 1775, and Drum Major of Col. Bullard's regiment in 1777, located in Boston in 1780 as a trader. He sold tea, depreciated Continental money, state notes and loan certificates. In 1785, the war being over, he conceived the idea of interesting the inhabitants of the town in a musical project and in June his Mufick Gallery, called also "The Orcheftra," a building of some size, was begun "at the bottom of the Common" near the Mall. In August he advertised it as "The Pantheon where Vocal and Inftrumental Mufick will be performed." Concerts were to be given every Thursday evening until the hall was completed. Mr. Eaton's "young attempt to promote innocent amufement" as he called it, was not a success, and ended in September with an attachment served by the deputy sheriff. He continued in business as an auctioneer until 1811.

In the eighteenth century, prior to the Revolution and after, the Common was the popular recreation ground of the townspeople and its neighborhood, then as now, was the natural site for places of public entertainment. Mr. Pool, the first American exhibitor of equestrian feats, located in 1786 "near the Mall where he erected a Menage at very confiderable expenfe, with feats for ladies and gentlemen." The performance commenced at five in the afternoon, tickets were sold at the principal taverns, and no dogs were allowed.

The failure of Eaton's Pantheon was due in great part to the controversy as to allowing dramatic exhibitions, for in March, 1750, the General Court had passed an act "For preventing and avoiding the many and great mifchiefs which arife from public ftage-plays, interludes, and other theatrical entertainments" and in spite of several efforts this had not yet been repealed. This prohibition was reenacted in 1784, and a vigorous effort in 1792 to repeal it having failed, the friends of the drama built the New Exhibition Room in Board Alley (now Hawley Street). This was a theatre, except in name, held five hundred persons, and was open from August 10, 1792, until the middle of June, 1793, when the building was taken down. Plays, including *Romeo and Juliet*, *Hamlet*, *Othello*, and Otway's *Venice Preserved*, were given as "Moral Lectures" though not without indignant protest from the anti-theatre party. The success of the Board Alley Theatre led to the erection in 1793 of the Boston Theatre in Federal Street, a substantial brick building designed by Bulfinch, who was one of the trustees. Boston's theatrical history began with its opening, February 3, 1794. Its success and the party politics of the day resulted in the project of a rival theatre.

As early as 1792 Charles Stuart Powell had been giving dramatic entertainments at Concert Hall. He was connected with the Board Alley enterprise and had been the first manager of the Federal Street theatre. Encouraged by his friends he issued early in 1796 proposals for building a new theatre to be called the Hay-Market, possibly because it was to be located just beyond the hay-market of the day, or after London's famous theatre, or in reference to one and deference to the other. It was advertised on its opening as *Hay-Market Theatre*. The land on the southerly part of the Sheafe-Holbrook lot (now 178 and 179 Tremont Street) at the back of which the Sheafe brew house and stable had stood, was purchased of Israel Hatch, one of the projectors, and the erection of the theatre begun.

Hatch Tavern   Hay-Market Theatre Head Place and House

In the *Columbian Centinel* of November 20, 1796, is a reference to the Sheafe mansion: Mr. J. B. Baker advertises the *Hay-Market Hotel* and "Informs his Friends and the Public, that he has taken that large and convenient Houſe lately occupied by Col. Israel Hatch, at the bottom of the Mall, for the purpose of improving it as a *Public Hotel and Tavern*," etc., etc., "in the vicinity of the New Theatre."

The Hay-Market, larger than its Federal Street rival, was a great wooden pile which proudly overtopped every other building in Boston, and had three tiers of boxes, gallery, pit, and drawing-rooms. In the summer Mr. Powell visited England to secure attractions and on December 26, 1796, the Hay-Market opened with a strong company in Mrs. Cowley's play *The Belle's Strategem*. The play was a success, others followed and the prosperity of the Hay-Market stimulated the manager and actors of the rival Federal Street to their utmost endeavors. The most intense jealousy existed between all connected with the two theatres. The stockholders of the older theatre being men of wealth spared no expense, reduced their scale of prices, bought out or papered the performances and sought to injure the new theatre in every way. This rivalry was so bitter that the Hay-Market proprietors took extra precautions against any attempt to set fire to their big wooden building, for a conflagration would menace the south end of the town. The public were warned that after 9 p.m., besides a night watch, there were on the north, south, and east of the building two spring-guns and four man-traps.

When Archibald Robertson, the Scotch artist and drawing-master of Washington Allston, was in Boston he painted on September 28, 1798, a water-color showing the Hay-Market Theatre. This became the property of John Howard Payne, the homeless author of *Home, Sweet Home,* who in his youth had acted with success on the Boston stage. After Payne's death it was bought in the sale of his effects by Mr. Foster of New Jersey from whom it passed to the Boston

Robertson's view of Common Street (Tremont Street) in 1798

Public Library. It is here reproduced from the original. The arch on the right is the gate to the Common opposite West Street. To the left is the old haymarket and scales. Behind the nearest load of hay is the tavern known as the Hay-Market Hotel, formerly the house and inn of Col. Israel Hatch, and beyond is the Hay-Market Theatre. The smaller building opposite is Billy Foster's house, now the site of the Little

Building. Under the trees to the right are the waters of the Back Bay.

On Monday Evening, June 4, 1798, Mr. Barrett, the actor-manager, at his benefit at the Hay-Market Theatre sang Robert Treat Paine's song, *Adams and Liberty*, which had been published in Boston three days before. It was then advertised and afterward widely known as "The Boston Patriotic Song." Mr. Barrett

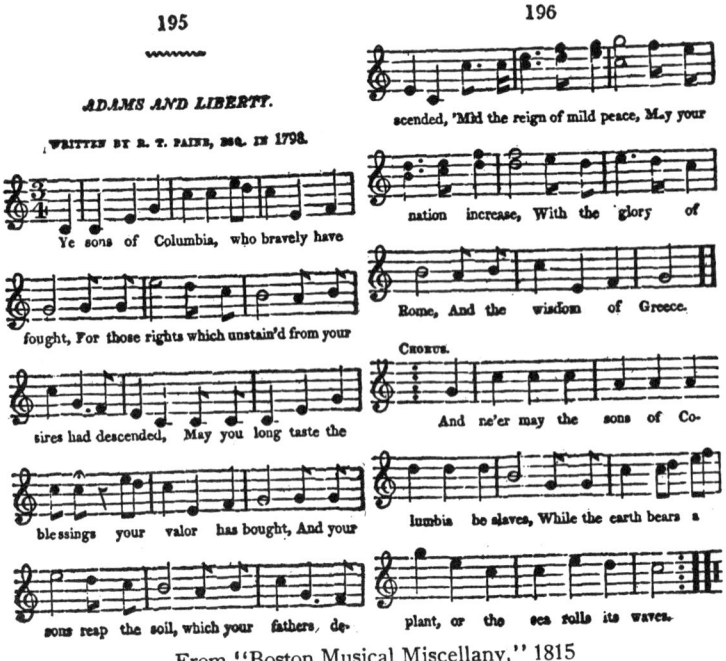

ADAMS AND LIBERTY.

WRITTEN BY R. T. PAINE, ESQ. IN 1798.

Ye sons of Columbia, who bravely have fought, For those rights which unstain'd from your sires had descended, May you long taste the blessings your valor has bought, And your sons reap the soil, which your fathers, descended, 'Mid the reign of mild peace, May your nation increase, With the glory of Rome, And the wisdom of Greece.

CHORUS.

And ne'er may the sons of Columbia be slaves, While the earth bears a plant, or the sea rolls its waves.

From "Boston Musical Miscellany," 1815

also sang on this occasion "The Philadelphia Patriotic Song"—*Hail! Columbia*; and Mrs. Catherine Graupner sang, "accompanied on the Hautboy by Mr. Graupner." When President Adams attended the Hay-Market on June 5, 1799, John Hodgkinson, the eminent actor-vocalist and manager of the theatre, sang *Adams and Liberty*. This patriotic use of John Stafford Smith's music became so popular that when Key's *Star-Spangled Banner* appeared in Baltimore in 1814 it was labelled "to be sung to the tune of *Adams and Liberty*."

Theatre advertisements of the period and for years afterward read *Doors to be opened at 5, and the Curtain to rise at 6 o'clock precisely*. The receipts falling off, Hodgkinson closed the theatre July 4, 1799. The Hay-Market was opened the next season and the two following for occasional performances by strolling companies, but it paid the proprietors so poorly (for Boston could not then support two theatres) that in February, 1803, it was offered for sale at auction under the condition that it be torn down and the materials removed within sixty days. The land was also sold at auction on June 1. This was the year when Charles Street at the foot of the Common was laid out.

The purchasers of the theatre site were John Amory, the owner of Concert Hall, and his sister, Rebecca Lowell, children and heirs of John Amory of Newbury Street (now Washington). Rebecca was the wife of John Lowell, prominent as a lawyer and writer and noted for his benevolence. Four brick houses were erected in 1803, the two southerly being Mrs. Lowell's portion. Just to the south was a ten-foot passage (now Head Place) which turned at right angles and divided her lot in the rear. John Amory, her brother, had the two northern houses. The total frontage on Common Street was one hundred and twenty feet with a depth of one hundred and sixty-two feet. To secure a clear title it was necessary to obtain deeds from all owning proprietors' shares in the vanished Hay-Market Theatre, each conveying 1/49th for $150. The list shows not only the business standing but also the political leaning of each grantor, for the Hay-Market proprietors were for the most part Jacobins while those of the surviving theatre were Federalists. These four brick houses were pioneers in antedating any group of houses facing the Common on either Beacon, Park, or Common Streets.

In 1806 the most southerly of the four houses, now 179 Tremont Street, was purchased by Mary Langdon, daughter of Thomas Walley, a wealthy Boston merchant. Her husband, John Langdon, born in 1747, had in his youth been apprenticed with Henry Knox to the booksellers, Wharton & Bowes. Like Knox he became an artillery officer in the Revolution and resigned in 1778 when a captain in Colonel Henry Jackson's regiment, and like Knox he had, previous to the war, started a book and stationer's shop in Cornhill. His fourth child, Abigail Langdon, married Giles Lodge in 1799. They were the grandparents of Henry Cabot Lodge, the present senior senator from Massachusetts.

As Mrs. Langdon passed to and fro from her shopping "down town" she must have watched in 1809 the erection of the Park Street church with its graceful spire, and seen in 1811 and thereafter the building of the continuous row of brick dwellings that continued northward from the Amory-Lowell block to West Street. Charles Bulfinch was the architect of these aristocratic houses long known as Colonnade Row, though dubbed by the less favored as "Cape Cod Row." Mrs. Langdon's house is listed in the directories of the time as No. 28 Colonnade Row. During the war of 1812 the corner of the Common opposite her house was used as a parking place for artillery. The street in front of her house, long called Common Street, became Tremont Street in 1829, although after the jubilation at the visit of General Lafayette in 1824 it had been unofficially known as Fayette Place.

On the death of Mrs. Langdon in 1835 the house, then numbered 116 Tremont Street, was purchased by Josiah Stickney, a man of large business interests and an enthusiast in horticulture, for he purchased the old Latin School House in School Street, the present lower end of the Parker House,

Colonnade Row in 1860

and offered it as a site for the Horticultural Hall that was in 1845 built on it. In this year he sold his house to Eliphalet Baker, a dry goods merchant, from whom it passed in 1853 to William Shattuck Lincoln, a well

Colonnade Row in 1858. Spire of Hollis Street Church. Hotel Pelham

known merchant who resided in the house, then renumbered 179, until his death in 1855, when his heirs sold it to William D. Sohier of Cohasset, a prominent Boston lawyer. In 1858 Mr. Sohier bought the adjoining house on the north, No. 178, and joined it to No. 179, making a double house, which he occupied as a residence. The next house to the north in the Amory-Lowell group, No. 177, was long owned by the Codman family, and in 1861 was the residence of J. Amory Codman.

After the death of William D. Sohier in 1868 his widow lived in the double house until 1872. The great

fire of that year, with
the consequent scarcity
of buildings, drove business
into what had
previously been an aristocratic
residential section,
and one by one
the houses of Colonnade
Row became shops,
while their former occupants moved into the fast developing
Back Bay section or elsewhere. In 1877 the
Sohier houses were torn down and a six-story business
block, known as *The Knickerbocker Building* was built
on the site. This block was in turn demolished in June,
1916, to be replaced by the ten-story building erected
by Mr. Charles H. Ditson for the Oliver Ditson Company
and occupied by it since September, 1917.

New Winthrop House, 1852
(No. 179 Tremont Street at the left)

Colonnade Row in 1844

Oliver Ditson

Charles H. Ditson

FIFTY YEARS MORE

In 1860, Mr. Ditson established in Cincinnati, Mr. John Church, a young man who had been with him from boyhood. The business successfully launched was in 1871 sold to Mr. Church, and is now well known as The John Church Company.

In 1864, two young men, Mr. P. J. Healy and Mr. George W. Lyon, were established in Chicago by the capital of Oliver Ditson & Co., under the now honored name of Lyon & Healy.

John Church

On March 4, 1867, the firm purchased the music plates, stock and good-will of Firth, Son & Co. of New York City. This led at once to the establishment of a branch house in the metropolis, under the management of Oliver Ditson's eldest son, Charles, with the firm name of Chas. H. Ditson & Co.

P. J. Healy

After remaining a few months at 563 Broadway,

where Firth, Son & Co. had been located, more spacious quarters were taken at 711 Broadway. The purchase by the parent house of the music catalog and business of Wm. Hall & Son of New York, in 1875, and of J. L. Peters of New York, in 1877, necessitated the taking of more spacious quarters, in 1878, at 843 Broadway.

In 1883, the property at the southwest corner of Broadway and Eighteenth Street was purchased and the Ditson Building erected. Here at 867 Broadway the firm remained until the constant uptown trend or retail trade led to the erection of a new Ditson Building at 8-10-12 East 34th Street. Into these handsome quarters the firm moved in 1907, just forty years after its establishment.

8–12 East 34th Street

In 1875, the purchase of the catalog of Lee & Walker of Philadelphia, led to the opening of a branch house in that city under the management of another son, James Edward Ditson, under the firm name of J. E. Ditson & Co.

In 1879, the stock and music plates of G. Andre & Co. of Philadelphia, were purchased.

In 1881, the uptown trend of business led to the removal from 922 to 1228 Chestnut Street. In the same year occurred the death of Mr. J. E. Ditson.

In 1890, the entire catalog, stock and music plates of F. A. North & Co. of Philadelphia, were purchased. In 1910, changed conditions of business led to the discontinuance of the Philadelphia branch house.

In 1877, the purchase of the catalog and good-will of G. D. Russell & Co. of Boston, and the constantly expanding business of the parent Boston house compelled the taking of the adjoining store at No. 449 Washington Street, which had been erected expressly as an addition to No. 451.

449-451 Washington Street

With the issue of December 21, 1878, Oliver Ditson & Co. ceased to publish *Dwight's Journal of Music* and established the *Monthly Musical Record*, which in 1898 was succeeded by the *Musical Record*, a high-class magazine under the brilliant editorship of Philip Hale.

In October, 1898, the issue was begun of a pocket-size monthly magazine to bulletin the publications of the house, under the name *Music Review*.

In January, 1901, this magazine was combined with the *Musical Record* under the name *Musical Record & Review*, with Thomas Tapper as editor. After more than two years' issue in its enlarged form another combination was made by the purchase from the Hatch Music Co. of Philadelphia of *The Musician*. The smaller magazine was dropped and the new magazine in its present form issued under Mr. Tapper's editorship from November, 1903, to August, 1907, when he was succeeded by Mr. W. J. Baltzell, who has conducted the magazine ever since.

On December 21, 1888, Oliver Ditson passed away at the ripe age of seventy-seven. He had been not only a great music publisher, but for twenty years President of the Continental Bank, director in various institutions, a constant though unostentatious promotor of good works in others, and the quiet helper of many a struggling musician. On Sunday Afternoon, December 23, he was buried from Trinity Church, the Rev. Phillips Brooks officiating. Mr. J. C. D. Parker, the son of his early employer, presided at the organ. The surviving partners, John C. Haynes, Charles H. Ditson, and the executors of Oliver Ditson's estate, then organized the corporation, Oliver Ditson Company, with Mr. Haynes as President.

In 1891, larger quarters being needed, the extensive

Oliver Ditson

property at 453-463 Washington Street, known as the Dexter Building, was leased and occupied until 1901.

Mr. Charles H. Ditson having erected a modern ten-story building at 451 Washington Street, on the site of the five-story building erected by his father in 1857 for Oliver Ditson & Co., the business was in 1901 moved into it. Changing conditions

453–463 Washington Street

and the necessity of still larger quarters caused the removal on January 25, 1904, to the new building constructed for its special needs at 150 Tremont Street, facing Boston Common. Upon the death May 3, 1907, of Mr. John C. Haynes, after sixty-two years connection with the house, the Presidency of the corporation and the direction of

451↑Washington St.

John C. Haynes

its great interests devolved naturally and fittingly upon the son of the founder, Mr. Charles Healy Ditson.

The eight-story building at 150 Tremont Street, proving too cramped, Mr. Ditson erected a larger and thoroughly modern ten-story building at 178-179 Tremont Street, where not only the specific requirements of the various departments were well cared for, but provision was made for inevitable growth and expansion. Into this permanent home the business was moved in September, 1917.

150 Tremont Street

CHRONOLOGY OF
THE OLIVER DITSON COMPANY

1783 Ebenezer Battelle opens the Boston Book-Store at 8 State Street.
1785 Benjamin Guild purchases Battelle's music and circulating library.
1786 Guild moves to 59 Cornhill (Washington Street).
1792 Guild dies and William Pinson Blake continues the business.
1796 William Pelham succeeds Blake at 59 Cornhill.
1804 William Blagrove takes Pelham's business at 5 School Street.
1808 Blagrove moves to 61 Cornhill (Washington Street).
1809 Blagrove moves to 3 School Street.
1811 Samuel H. Parker succeeds Blagrove at 3 School Street.
1811 Oliver Ditson born in Boston on October 20.
1815 Parker moves to 4 Cornhill (Washington Street).
1818 Parker moves to 12 Cornhill (Washington Street).
1823 Oliver Ditson enters the employ of Colonel S. H. Parker.
1825 Parker moves to 164 Washington Street.
1826 Oliver Ditson becomes an apprentice to Isaac R. Butts.
1833 Fire destroys Parker's store, November 1.
1834 Parker reopens in January at 10 School Street.
1834 Parker moves in April to 141 Washington Street.
1834 Parker moves in December to 107 Washington Street.
1835 Oliver Ditson begins to publish and copyright music at 107 Washington Street.
1836 Firm of Parker & Ditson formed on April 5.

1835–1838    1838–1844    1844–1857    1857–1877

1838 Parker & Ditson move to 135 Washington Street.
1842 Oliver Ditson acquires the interests of Samuel H. Parker.
1844 Oliver Ditson moves to 115 Washington Street.
1845 John C. Haynes enters the employ of Oliver Ditson.
1857 Oliver Ditson & Co. formed by admitting John C. Haynes.
1857 Mr. Ditson erects building at 277 (now 451) Washington Street.
1858 Oliver Ditson & Co. take over *Dwight's Journal of Music.*
1860 Mr. Ditson establishes John Church in Cincinnati.
1864 Mr. Ditson establishes Lyon & Healy in Chicago.
1867 Chas. H. Ditson & Co. established in New York.
1875 J. E. Ditson & Co. established in Philadelphia.
1877 Store at 449 Washington Street taken as an addition to No. 451.
1881 Death of James Edward Ditson.
1888 Death of Oliver Ditson, December 21.
1889 Oliver Ditson Company incorporated, John C. Haynes, Pres.
1891 Removal to 453-463 Washington Street.
1901 Removal to new ten-story building at 451 Washington Street.
1904 Removal to new and larger building at 150 Tremont Street.
1907 Death of John C. Haynes, May 3.
1907 Charles H. Ditson becomes President.
1916 Mr. Ditson begins erection of building at 178-179 Tremont Street.
1917 Removal to new building at 178-179 Tremont Street.

1877-1891   1891-1901   1901-1904   1904-1917

Ditson Building, 178–179 Tremont Street

THE DITSON BUILDING

THE focus of modern Boston's shopping activity is at the corner of Tremont and Boylston Streets, where converge the currents of vivid life from hotels, theatres and subways. Facing the Common on Tremont Street, within a stone's throw of this teeming corner, rises the

stately façade of the most recent among the city's notable structures; it is the splendid new home of the Oliver Ditson Company. White marble was the material selected, as being worthy of the art to which the building is devoted; and the style chosen was an adaptation of the Renaissance. As seems fitting, both because of proportions and of the purposes of the various stories, the first and second indicate, by ornamentation, their use for music, the carved decorations between the windows in the third story being of musical instruments surrounding panels that contain the names of composers to whose work these instruments are appropriate, for instance: with the name of Gounod are the drum and trumpets of the March in *Faust;* with Verdi, the guitar, symbolic of Italian lyricism; with Wagner, the horns and tragic mask; with Bizet, the tambourines and castanets of Carmen's dance; with Beethoven, the violin, and with Schubert, the lyre of song. The columned upper stories dignify this portion of the building, as it contains the Memorial Room to Oliver Ditson, besides the various managerial offices. Notably handsome is the bronze finish by Tiffany of the show windows and entrances, as well as the verde antique panels above. The elevator doors and grills are likewise of bronze, and the entrance vestibule is in antique Siena marble. The interior of the building fully bears out in beauty and convenience the promise of the exterior.

Above the sub-basement, which contains the heating-plant and other vital mechanism of a great modern building, is a high studded, airy basement, which houses a complete working stock of books, both American and imported; and here are carried also the complete octavo publications of the great Ditson catalogue, now including more than 13,000 numbers.

The street floor is given over entirely to the retail music store, which is without question one of the largest

Retail Music Department — Street floor

and most perfectly appointed in this or any other city. It is remarkable for its spaciousness, its flood of light and the elegant detail observed in all its fittings. A mezzanine balcony, with ornamental railing, surrounds three sides of the store, to afford accessible accommodation for the large stock which must be carried to serve retail needs.

The convenience of customers has been everywhere

considered in arranging the various departments. On the right as one enters, books in the field of musical literature are displayed in handsome cases, and adjoining is found the vocal department; on the same side but farther towards the rear is the piano music. In the centre of the store is a large elliptical counter given over to the sale of octavo music, including choral works from every publisher in the country. It may be safely stated that organists and choirmasters of Boston have never found so comfortable a place for the arduous task of music selection as is offered them here. To the left of the entrance is the important department devoted to the sale of foreign music, and farther to the rear, beyond

Victor Department — Second floor

the elevators, is a commodious section for the band and orchestra department. The pneumatic cash system insures prompt service. A desirable innovation is a sound-proof room, where those who desire to try over music at the piano can do so, undisturbed and undisturbing. At the rear entrance of the store is a shipping-room for light packages, the freight and express packages being shipped from the basement.

On the second story, reached by two elevators, is the department for the sale of Victor Talking Machines, which occupies this entire floor. Numerous small rooms in which customers may try out records surround two sides of the main salesroom; they are as

Manager of the Victor Department

nearly sound-proof as may be, airy, all open to the daylight, and Persian rugs add to their comfort and beauty.

The third floor is devoted to the needs of the wholesale and jobbing departments. The large amount of sheet music stock carried for this purpose is kept ac-

Wholesale Music Department — Third floor

cording to a convenient and dust-proof arrangement, which is a successful application of the well-known Tindale Music Cabinet system on an extensive scale. This specially planned equipment makes it possible to handle the large volume of orders in much less time and with a fraction of the labor involved in the old method.

On the fourth floor is the retail salesroom for musical instruments. Here can be found every instrument

Retail Instrument Department — Fourth floor

Instrument Department — Fourth floor

used in band or orchestra, from the most expensive violin and harp down to the Chinese drum employed by the percussion player, as well as all the small accessories and devices which instrumental performers require. It is safe to say that no more admirable plan for the display and sale of musicians' supplies is to be found in this country. Falling in admirably with the restful decorative scheme is the display of harps—the most beautiful of instruments to the eye—ranging from the quaint little Irish harp up to Lyon & Healy's most superb modern production. The wholesale de-

Repair Department — Fifth floor

partment for the sale of instruments is located on the fifth floor; and here also, in a spacious, well-lighted workroom, expert masters of their delicate craft give first aid and final cure to all musical instruments which have fallen temporarily out of joint or out of tune.

The front of the sixth story is occupied by the large force employed in the bookkeeping department, and here also is the handsomely furnished and oak-panelled office of the Treasurer. The rear of this floor gives further space for the storage of musical merchandise.

The seventh, eighth and ninth stories are rented to

Office of the Treasurer — Sixth floor

tenants, for whose convenience a separate entrance from the street and two special elevators are provided.

The tenth and top story is certainly a fitting culmination to this fine establishment. Here are housed in luxury the various offices devoted to the managerial and mechanical activities of a great publishing firm.

Central Office — Tenth floor

Stepping from the elevator one enters a large square apartment, oak-panelled to the ceiling and lighted by an ample skylight. This gives accommodation to clerks connected with the various offices. Across the front of the building is a suite of three rooms: to the right on leaving the elevator is the private office of the General Manager; the central office is the President's

Office of the General Manager—Tenth floor

Room; and the one beyond is the private room of the Musical Editor, wherein a handsome Steinway grand piano is conspicuous among the professional attributes. These rooms are as handsome in decoration and furnishing as good taste can suggest and money can procure. Panelled to the ceiling in Jacobean quartered oak, with furniture specially designed and made to match, they certainly represent the last word in modern office equipment.

Office of the Musical Editor and Publishing Manager

But without doubt the crowning feature of the entire building is the room set apart for the use of the President, for directors' meetings, and similar gatherings. Here, too, the woodwork is of dark quartered oak and there is an ornamental English plaster ceiling. The floor is of dull red Mercer tiles and the small-paned casement windows, affording a beautiful view over the Common, form a slightly rounded front to the room. The two side walls are occupied by glassed-in bookcases. The rear wall contains a fireplace of Botticino marble, topped by a carved oak mantel, in the centre of which, surrounded by a richly carved frame built into the panelling, is a portrait of the late Oliver Ditson, the founder of the house. The flanking pilasters of the

President's Room and Library

frame are carved with pendants of flowers and fruit, while above are two corbels representing respectively medieval and classic music; this carving is by Mr. I. Kirchmayer. Below the shelf of the mantel, partially concealed in foliage, is a Greek motto ascribed to Socrates, which may be translated as follows: "Make music and work making it." No more appropriate motto for this first of American music houses could be discovered. In the centre of the ceiling is a silver Flemish chandelier. All the hardware throughout this story is of silver finish, and the floors in all these rooms are adorned with Oriental rugs. The remainder of the rooms are other offices for the editorial staff, the office of the Editor of *The Musician*, the private and general offices for the manager of the printing department and his large staff of workers, and the private office for the head of the band and orchestra department. In pursuance of the policy of the house to provide every comfort for those in its employ, there is a fully equipped rest room on this floor for the women employees.

The building was planned by Edward W. Briggs and Clarence A. Woodman, of the Oliver Ditson Company, and financed by its President, Charles H. Ditson, son of Oliver Ditson. The architects were Townsend, Steinle, and Haskell, of New York, and C. Howard Walker and Son, of Boston. To the latter firm should be given credit for the façade and the unique interior fittings and decorations.

The "tall and solitary bachelors' apartment house,"

Beacon Street from the roof of the Ditson Building

referred to on page 1, as standing almost on the site of William Blaxton's hut, is conspicuous in the view of Beacon Street taken from the roof of the Ditson Building, looking northwest across the Common. The snowy heights of Medford are beyond. The "Soldiers Monument" spoken of in the Prefatory Note appears in this picture and in the one that follows, which was taken from the roof of the bachelors' apartment house at No. 48 Beacon Street.

Tremont Street from West Street to Boylston

This view of Tremont Street shows the transformation of Colonnade Row from West Street and the Lawrence Building at the left to the Ditson Building at the right, directly over the Army and Navy Monument. Next to the Lawrence Building is the one previously erected in 1903–1904 for the Oliver Ditson Company at 150 Tremont Street. Since their removal in 1917 two additional floors have been added. A few of the dwelling houses of the once fashionable Row appear in this picture little changed. A bit of the historic "Frog Pond" fills the lower left-hand corner of the picture.

The view of the Back Bay district taken from the

Back Bay district from tenth floor of Ditson Building

central upper windows of the Ditson Building shows in the foreground the southwest corner of the Common, the Public Garden beyond it, and a group of church spires—massive Trinity at the left, near it the New Old South, Arlington Street nearer by, a little to the right that of Central Church and the Florentine tower of the First Baptist Church, with the spire of the First Church in Boston farther to the right. Across the Charles River the buildings of the Institute of Technology show white in the sunshine.

The view of the recently enlarged State House was

taken from the roof of the Ditson Building. The obelisk of Bunker Hill Monument shows faintly over the right wing. The building on the right with two new upper stories in process of construction is that recently vacated by the Oliver Ditson Company.

State House from the roof of the Ditson Building

The view of Tremont Street taken in March, 1918, may be contrasted with the drawing on page 50, showing the same section in 1800. It shows again the transformation of the once quiet and exclusive Colonnade Row to a busy shopping district. On the site of the Ditson Building in the foreground the first group of brick houses facing the Common was erected in 1803, and Park Street Church, seen at the left, was built in 1809. The section of the Common in the foreground was, in 1812, a parking place for artillery. Beneath it and the once quiet Central Burying Ground adjacent now rumbles the ceaseless traffic of the Subway.

Tremont Street in March, 1918

Other changes as radical will doubtless follow, and some years hence the irregular sky line between the old and new Ditson buildings, the first to rise above their neighbors, will doubtless be filled by an even row of structures worthy of their unique position.

OFFICERS AND DIRECTORS OF THE OLIVER DITSON COMPANY

President
CHARLES H. DITSON

Secretary and Treasurer
EDWARD W. BRIGGS

Directors
CHARLES H. DITSON
EDWARD S. CRAGIN
CLARENCE A. WOODMAN

Stockholders

CHARLES H. DITSON and ESTATE OF OLIVER DITSON

EDWARD W. BRIGGS
CLIFFORD C. CHAPMAN
EDWARD S. CRAGIN
WILLIAM A. FISHER
JOHN B. HAUSWIRTH
HARRY L. HUNT
HENRY MACLAREN

CHARLES F. MANNEY
WILLIAM J. O'MEARA
WILLIAM J. REILLY
THOMAS H. ROLLINSON
JAMES A. SMITH
HENRY A. WINKELMAN
CLARENCE A. WOODMAN

HONORABLE MENTION

THE appreciation of the house for its employees and the esteem in which it is held by them is shown by the names of those given below, who have been connected with the business for five years and upwards.

More than Fifty Years

Charles H. Ditson
*Edward S. Cragin

Arthur B. Flint
*Frank H. Gould

William Holmes

More than Forty-five Years

Charles B. Donovan
Charles B. Hollis

Miss Josephine L. Rossiter
Windsor C. Wright

More than Forty Years

Edward Kirk
*J. Fred Olfers
*Joseph M. Priaulx
Roland B. Winterton
Clarence A. Woodman

More than Thirty-five Years

Clifford C. Chapman
Gus Enders
*Edward Moisson
*John K. Morehouse
Henry Schlimper
Henry A. Winkelman

More than Thirty Years

Robert P. Anderson
Henry Beach
John H. Burke
John J. Connell
James L. Fitzgerald
George W. Furniss
*Joseph Glassmacher
John B. Hauswirth
William S. Hollis
Henry MacLaren
John Miller
Frank Oeffenger
*William J. O'Meara
William J. Reilly
Thomas H. Rollinson
*Floyd Schoonmacher
Jacob Wronker
*Miss Mary E. Woodward

More than Twenty-five Years

Edward W. Briggs
*Louis R. Dressler
Harry Fisher
*Henry Harris
*Fred Morlock
August Piesendel
Max Pulverman
*Charles Rumsby
George H. Shirley
James A. Smith
John Stromberg
Elmer J. Swett
*Miss Clara Thomas
*Miss Elizabeth Ward

More than Twenty Years

John W. Chandler
*Louis H. Fichten
William A. Fisher
Harry Haney
James Hermitage
*Harry L. Hunt
Benjamin K. Little
Charles F. Manney
John O. Martin
*William J. Moore
Fred W. Schmidt
*Frank Sinclair
Henry T. Travis

More than Fifteen Years

Mrs. Mabel Bean
*Miss Amelia Bishop
Charles E. Durgin
*William Froese
John Frey
Charles Hellman
Frank Huxley
*Miss Mary C. Jennings

Herman Knauber
Henry O. Ladd
Otto A. Piesendel
Miss V. Clyde Robbins
Miss Annie E. Rose
Frank Sala
*John F. Scott
Louis Wilmot

More than Ten Years

William Adams
Winton J. Baltzell
Charles E. Beagley
Walter F. Blaser
Stephen S. Bruen
John C. Canavan
*Paul E. W. Carlson
*Harry J. Eaton
James H. Fernald
Miss Inez Hall
William R. Hawes
*Alfred C. Hippman
*William Juneman

Miss Olga Jansen
*Charles Kindt
Leslie A. Martell
*Charles Morlock
Miss Lillian Neal
J. La Motte Osgood
Charles F. Pidgeon
F. Wendell Pierce
James Reardon
Carl Sander
*Fred Spingler
Frank Welch
Miss Eva E. White

More than Five Years

Edward F. Andrews
Miss May Beck
Miss Carrie Bowers
Walter C. Brice
*Carl Davider
*John Davidson
Miss Anna E. Drew
Charles Farley
Frank W. Fernald
*Miss Anna Ford
*Leon Gardner

*Thomas Gray
Oscar C. Henning
*Miss Ruth Keller
Miss Mary F. Kennedy
*William Kidd
*William Lind
*Joseph May
*Miss Camille Michaelis
Miss Eleanor Murray
Frederick Newall
*Miss Johanna Nordheim

Joseph Rafalee
*Charles T. Rouss
*Grover Rouss
*Miss Julia E. Salvatore
Miss Annabelle Scott
John Secord

Miss Honora Sheriden
*James Sockwell
*Harry Van Wagenen
*Miss Elizabeth Werschmidt
Miss May White
Miss Louise Wilkinson

Ernest Wurlitzer

WITH THE COLORS

Robert B. Beers —*Army*
David S. Blandon — *Navy*
Walter Blaser —*Army*
Benni Busoni —*Army*
John W. Canavan — *Navy*
Joseph O. N. Carlson —*Army*
Clifford L. Carter —*Army*
Alden Clark —*Army* (Died in service)
Warren Coleman — *Navy*
*Carl Davider —*Army*
*George De Martins —*Laboratory Dept.*
*Harry J. Eaton —*Army*
Herman Flick —*Army*
*Leon Gardner —*Army*
Paul Kachele —*Army*
George Kerr — *Navy*
Thomas Killduff —*Navy*
*William Lind —*Army*
James Loughlin —*Army*
*George Parker —*Army*
Wilfred F. Pierpont —*Army*
*Grover Rouss —*Army*
Carl Sander —*Army*
*Gustav Stultz —*Army*
Charles Sullivan — *Navy*
Joseph Sweeney —*Army*
Edwin W. Staniland—*Army*

* With Chas. H. Ditson & Co.

INDEX

	Page
Abt, Franz	47
Academy of Music Orchestra	41
Adams and Liberty	62, 63
Adams, President	62
Alboni	44
Allston, Washington	60
American Harmony, The Holden	14
Amory, John	63
Andre, G., & Co.	71
Arlington	xiv
Athenæum Press	3
Autocrat of the Breakfast Table	xiv
Bach, J. S.	8, 47
Back Bay	xiv, xv, 62, 67, 94
Baltzell, W. J.	73
Battelle's Boston Bookstore	14, 22, 23
Battelle, Col. Ebenezer	22, 23, 76
Bay Psalm Book, The	3, 4
Beacon Street	xiv, 64, 92, 93
Beethoven	11, 40
Billings, William	xv, 11–13
Blagrove, William	24, 25, 76
Blake, William Pinson	23, 76
Blaxton, Rev. William	xv, 1, 93
Board Alley Theatre	58, 59
Booksellers and Bookshops	1, 14, 19, 20–29, 64
Boston	
Settlement of	1
Naming of	1
Purchase of	xv
Population of	6, 30, 35, 38
Early Book and Music Shops in	19–30, 35
Early Music Publishing in	17–20, 26–28, 30, 35–37
Early Theatres	29, 58–63
First Railway Connections	38
First Trans-Atlantic Steamers	38

	Page
Boston Common	xiii–xvi, 49, 51–54, 56, 57, 61, 64–67, 74, 90, 92–96
Boston Symphony Orchestra	42
Bradford, Gov. William	38
Bradlee, Charles	27, 28
Brattle Square Church	4, 8, 9
Brattle, Thomas	8
Briggs, Edward W.	92
Brignoli	44
Buck, Dudley	46, 48
Bulfinch, Charles	58, 65
Bülow, von	45
Bull, Ole	32, 45, 46
Bunker Hill	xv
Cambridge	xiv, xv, 2, 3, 48, 52
Cambridge Short Tune	4
Carreño, Teresa	45
Chopin	32
Choirs	11, 14, 17, 35
Christ Church, Cambridge	xv
Church, John	70, 77
Codman, J. Amory	66
Collection of the Best Psalm Tunes Flagg	10
Colonial Literature	5
Colonnade Row	65–67, 93, 95
Columbian Songster, The	14
Concert Hall	16, 59, 63
Concerts of Music	15–17, 25, 27, 32, 33, 35, 36, 40–47, 57
Continental Harmony, The Billings	12
Copley, John Singleton	24
Copley, Mary	24
Coronation, Holden	13, 14
Cotton, Rev. John	2, 3
Dancing School	9
David, Oratorio of	36
Deblois, Gilbert	15

	Page		Page
Dedham	18	Graupner, Catherine	31, 62
Dibdin, Charles	18	Graupner, Gottlieb	
Dickson, James A.	28, 29		26, 27, 30, 31, 33, 34, 40, 62
Ditson Buildings	71, 72, 74–96	Graupner, John Henry Howard	
Ditson, Charles H.			34, 40
	67, 69, 70, 73–75, 77, 92	Grisi, Giulia	44
Ditson, Charles H., & Co.	70, 71, 77	*Grounds and Rules of Musick*	
Ditson, James Edward	71, 77	Walter	7
Ditson, J. E., & Co.	71, 72, 77	Guild, Benjamin	23, 76
Ditson, Joseph	31, 32		
Ditson, Oliver	28, 31–40	H<small>AIL</small>! *Columbia*	62
	47, 68, 70, 73, 76, 77, 80, 90	Hale, Philip	72
Ditson, Oliver, & Co.		Hall, William, & Son	71
	40, 43, 70, 72, 74, 77	Handel	8, 10, 11, 17, 18, 33, 36
Ditson, Oliver, Company		Handel and Haydn Society, The	
	67, 73, 76, 77, 79, 92, 93		26, 33, 34, 36, 42, 47
Ditson, Samuel	31	*Handel and Haydn Society*	
Dorchester	2	*Collection of Church Music*	33
Dunster, Rev. Henry	2	Harris, John	10, 11
Dwight, John S.	39, 43, 46	Harvard College	xiv, 2, 3, 22, 55
Dwight's Journal of Music		Harvard, Rev. John	3
	43, 44, 46, 72	Harvard Musical Association	42, 43
E<small>ATON</small>'s Musick Gallery	57, 58	Hatch, Israel	57, 59–61
Eichberg, Julius	46	Hawthorne, Nathaniel	32
Emerson, Ralph Waldo	xiv, 32	Haydn	18, 31
Enstone, Edward	9	Hay-Market Theatre	29, 49, 50, 59–64
Essipoff, Annette	45	Haynes, John C.	40, 73, 74, 77
		Healy, P. J.	70
F<small>ANEUIL</small> Hall	15	Henschel, Georg	43
Faneuil, Peter	15	Hermit of Shawmut, The	xv
Federal Street Theatre	29, 58–60	Higginson, Henry Lee	42
Fields, James T.	37	Hodgkinson, John	62
Firth, Son & Co.	70, 71	Holbrook, Albiah	53–57
Flagg, Josiah	10	Holbrook, Samuel	55, 56
Franklin, Benjamin	7	Holden, Oliver	13, 14
Franklin, J.	7	*Hollis Street*, Billings	12
Fuller, Margaret	38	Holmes, Oliver Wendell	xiv, 32
		Hook, James	18
G<small>ARRISON</small>, William Lloyd	32	Hutchinson, Anne	2, 37
Gericke, Wilhelm	43	Hutchinson, William	2
Germania Orchestra	41		
Gilmore, P. S.	46, 47	I<small>NDEPENDENT</small> Musical Society	16
Gluck	18		
Goldschmidt, Otto	44	J<small>OHNSON</small>, Isaac	1, 2
Gottschalk, Louis M.	45	Joy Street	xiv

	Page
K<small>ING'S</small> Chapel	8, 9, 15, 16, 32, 33, 50
Knotwork, Holbrook's	55–57
Knox, Henry	22, 27, 64
L<small>AFAYETTE</small>, General	xiv, 65
Lafayette Mall	xiv
Lang, B. J.	46
Langdon, Mrs. Mary Walley	64, 65
Larkin, E.	14
Lee & Walker	71
Liberty Song, The	17
Lind, Jenny	44
Lining out the Psalms	3, 4
Liszt	32
London Book-Store, The	17, 21, 22
Long Path	xiv
Longfellow, Henry W.	32
Louisburg Square	44
Lowell, Mrs. Rebecca Amory	63
Lyon, George W.	70
Lyon & Healy	70, 77, 86
Lyon, James	11
M<small>AC</small>D<small>OWELL</small>, Edward A.	48
MacMonnies	2
Mario, G.	44
Marseillaise, The	xiv
Mason, Lowell	33, 34
Mason, William	41
Mather, Dr. Cotton	8
Medfield, Billings	12
Mehlig, Anna	45
Mein, John	21
Mendelssohn Quintette Club	43
Messiah, The	33, 36
Monthly Musical Record	72
Morgan, George W.	46
Mozart	11, 18
Munroe, Francis and Parker	25, 26
Music Hall, Boston	41
Music in Miniature, Billings	12
Music Review	72
Music-shops	18–20, 24, 26–30, 35–37, 39, 40
Musical Fund Society	41

	Page
Musical Record	72
Musical Record and Review	72
Musician, The	73, 92
My Country, 'tis of thee	xvi
N<small>EWBURYPORT</small>	18
New England Psalm Singer, The Billings	11
New Exhibition Room	58
New Towne (Cambridge)	2, 3
New Way of Singing, The	7
New York	18, 35, 38, 47, 70, 71
Nikisch, Arthur	43
North, F. A., & Co.	72
Northampton	18
Note Singing, Innovation of	6
O<small>LD</small> Corner Bookstore	1, 37, 39, 40
Organ	xv, 8, 9, 45
Organ, Great	45
Organ, Holden's	13
P<small>AINE</small>, John K.	46, 48
Paine, Robert Treat	62
Pantheon, Eaton's	57, 58
Park Street Church	xvi, 9, 64, 95
Parker & Ditson	37, 39, 40, 76, 77
Parker, J. C. D.	73
Parker, Col. Samuel Hale	25–28, 33–35, 37, 76
Patriotic Music	17, 18, 62, 63
Patti, Adelina	44
Payne, John Howard	61
Peabody, Miss	38
Peace Jubilee of 1869	46
Peace Jubilee of 1872	47
Pelham, Peter	24
Pelham, Sarah	24
Pelham, William	23, 24, 76
Perkins, John	21
Peters, J. L.	71
Philadelphia	11, 18, 38, 71–73
Philharmonic Orchestra	42
Philharmonic Society, The	31
Phillips, Adelaide	44, 46

	Page		Page
Phillips, Wendell	xiv	Sivori, Ernesto	45
Plain and Easy Introduction		Smith, John Stafford	63
Tufts	6	Sohier, William D.	66
Pleyel	18	Soldiers and Sailors Monument	xiv
Powell, Charles Stuart	59, 60	Sontag, Henrietta	44
Price, William	24	Stage Coach Days	35
Psalm-Singer's Amusement, The		*St. Matthew Passion Music*	47
Billings	12	*Star-Spangled Banner, The*	63
Psalmody		Stickney, Josiah	65
	3, 4, 6–8, 10–14, 17, 20–22, 54	Stone Chapel, The	16
Public Garden, The	33, 41, 94	Storace, Stephen	18
Puritanism	2, 5	Stoughton Musical Society	13
		Stowe, Harriet Beecher	32
Queen's Chapel	8	Strauss, Johann	47
		Streeter, Father	9
Remenyi, Edward	45	Sumner, Charles	32
Revere, Paul	10		
Riverside Press	3	Tansur's *Royal Melody*	
Rivington, James	21	Compleat	21
Robertson, Archibald	60	Tapper, Thomas	72
Rosa, Carl	46	Thacher, Rev. Thomas	50, 51
Rosa, Parepa	44, 46	Thacher, Mrs.	50
Rubinstein, Anton	45	Thackeray	32
Rudersdorff, Hermine	47	Thalberg	45
Russell, G. D., & Co.	72	Thayer, Eugene	46
Russell, Henry	38	Thomas, Isaiah	14
Ryan, Thomas	9, 43	Thomas, Theodore	42
		Ticknor, William D.	37
Salem	18	*To Thee, O Country*, Eichberg	46
Sauret, Emile	45	Townsend, Steinle & Haskell	92
Schumann	32	Trimountaine	1
Secular Music, Early	4, 5, 14, 15, 18	Tuckerman, S. P.	46
Selby, William	16	Tufts, Rev. John	6
Sewall, Judge	7, 8, 52		
Shaw, Oliver	26	University Press	3
Sheafe, Jacob	50–53	*Urania*, Lyon	11
Sheafe, Margaret	50, 51	Urso, Camilla	45
Sheafe, Mehitable	50–52		
Sheafe, Sampson	51, 52	Valentine, F.	36
Shield, William	18	Vane, Sir Henry	2
Singing of Psalms a Gospel		Vieuxtemps, Henri	45
Ordinance, Cotton	3	Vocal Collections	11
Singing Master's Assistant, The		Von Hagen, P. A.	19
Billings	12		
Singing Schools	xvi, 7, 8, 13, 14	Walter, Rev. Thomas	4, 7

	Page		Page
Walker, C. Howard, & Sons	92	Winthrop, John	1, 2
Warville, Brissot de	17	Woodbridge, William C.	34
Washington, General	xv	Woodman, Clarence A.	92
Watertown	2	Worcester	14, 18
Webb, Henry	50	*Worcester Collection, The*	
Webb, Margaret	50	Holden	14
White Horse Tavern	53, 54		
Whittier, John G.	32	Yankee *Doodle*	xv
Wieniawski	45	*York Tune*	4, 7
Wilcox, John H.	46		
Wilhelmj, August	45	Zerrahn, Carl	42, 46
Windsor Tune	4, 7	Zeuner, Ch.	36